PRAISE FOR SAN FRANCISCO NOIR

"*San Francisco Noir* is a rare book that lets you step into a dream. The dream is film—all the seductive phantoms of film noir that have haunted us for decades—and by discovering so carefully and describing so memorably the loci of all these fantasies, Nathaniel Rich has written a fascinating work of criticism disguised as a guided tour around a great city. He puts you right in the middle of some wonderful movies—and what better travel book could there be?"

—Martin Scorsese

"Clearly the author has enjoyed himself, and his enthusiasm is contagious. He exudes a sort of film-buff certitude that you can't fake, but he tempers it with playful variations on a wised-up tone—sometimes cheekily Hitchcockian, sometimes hardboiled and Hammettesque . . . As a catalog of movie commentary, *San Francisco Noir* is uniquely serviceable . . . and as a guidebook is highly, refreshingly literary . . . His essays, while brief, pack in a lot: pithy critical analyses, informed surveys of the city's cultural history and some delectable lore about moviemaking tribulations . . . "

—Jonathan Kiefer,
The San Francisco Chronicle

"*San Francisco Noir* is both guide book and dream book. Following a meandering path from the Steinhart Aquarium to the site where the Paper Doll used to be, tracking remnants of the past while evoking what has irrevocably vanished, Nathaniel Rich charts the points where screen life and waking life intersect."

—Geoffrey O'Brien, author of *Hardboiled America:
Lurid Paperbacks and the Masters of Noir*

"Irresistible . . . A stylishly written, breezy, long-overdue companion to most of our films both noir and cryptonoir."

—David Kipen, *The San Francisco Chronicle*

W9-DDR-923

SAN FRANCISCO

Noir

Book design: Lisa Hamilton

First printing: January 2005. Printed in U.S.A.

Library of Congress Cataloging-in-Publication Data
Rich, Nathaniel, 1980-
San Francisco noir : the city in film noir from 1940 to the present / Nathaniel Rich.
p. cm.
Includes bibliographical references.
ISBN 1-892145-30-8
1. Film noir—United States—History and criticism. 2. San Francisco (Calif.)—In
motion pictures. I. Title.
PN1995.9.F54R48 2005
791.43'6556—dc22
2004026260

Published by The Little Bookroom
1755 Broadway, Fifth floor, New York, NY 10019
(212) 293-1643 Fax (212) 333-5374
editorial@littlebookroom.com

ISBN-13: 978-1-892145-30-7
ISBN-10: 1-892145-30-8

9 8 7 6 5 4 3 2

SAN FRANCISCO

Noir

The City in film noir from 1940 to the present

NATHANIEL RICH

THE LITTLE BOOKROOM
NEW YORK

CONTENTS

INTRODUCTION

A t a typical San Franciscan weekend gathering early last summer—a picnic in Golden Gate Park, balmy weather, dogs and people running around—a recent acquaintance politely asked me what in the world I meant by "San Francisco Noir." After all, she said, San Francisco is one of the happiest, most beautiful, and most romantic cities in the world. What, she wondered, could be so sinister or dark about this, the most radiant of American cities? I quickly scanned the rolling fields for some kind of countervailing evidence: a knifing in progress, perhaps, or a police chase or, at the very least, a discarded cigarette butt. Instead there were only all those overjoyed people and their dogs, splayed out on colorful blankets, or playing softball on the nearby ballfields, or strolling through the Cloud Forests of the Strybing Arboretum with peaceful expressions on their faces, pausing to smell sprigs of lemon verbena and Chilean Angel's Trumpets. I asked whether she had seen *The Maltese Falcon*. She had not. *Vertigo*? No. By the time I had finished mumbling something about Dashiell Hammett and Kim Novak and Rita Hayworth my friend was off in the middle of the field, chasing down a Frisbee.

Recently I found myself back at the park, only this time at night. It is a different park at night. It is very dark, and would be even darker were it not for the fog, which refracts the yellow light from the scattered streetlamps, spreading a sallow glow across empty fields and between crooked branches. The baseball fields, off of Seventh Avenue and Lincoln, lie in a depression; one has to walk down a short staircase from the street to reach them. On particularly foggy nights it's not even possible to see the bottom of the stairs, let alone the fields. Or whatever lies in the darkness beyond.

It is misleading to talk of a San Francisco fog. The city has many fogs, each one distinct. The fog that settles over the bay and the Golden Gate Bridge is majestic; the Twin Peaks fog is glum, like a thick wet blanket; the downtown fog is wispy and capricious, blotting out the Transamerica Pyramid one moment, and skidding off into the Bay the next; but the Golden Gate Park fog is the eeriest one of them all. It is a looming, shape-shifting mist that, especially at night, plays tricks of perception on anyone it engulfs. It is eerie not so much for what it conceals (a knobby tree trunk, a park bench, a twisting garden path, a baseball diamond) but for what one fears it *might* conceal. More than anything else it is this feeling—dread—that is the subject of film noir.

"Film noir" is itself an amorphous, foggy term. Coined by French film critic Nino Frank in 1946 and popularized by French critics Raymond Borde and Étienne Chaumeton in their 1955 study *Panorama du film noir américain*, the term describes, in its most narrow application, a series of American films made during World War II and in the years following, punctuated by violence and pervaded with a profound sense of dread and moral uncertainty. The heroes tend to be cynical, tough, and overwhelmed by sinister forces beyond their control. Stylistically, film noir is distinguished by its stark chiaroscuro cinematography, influenced in large part by German expressionism (many of film noir's greatest directors, including Fritz Lang, Otto Preminger, Billy Wilder, Robert Siodmak, and Edgar Ulmer had emigrated from Germany and Austria in the 1930s). Films are shot in black and white, lit for night, favor oblique camera angles and obsessive use of shadow, and, most importantly, take place in a city. Film noir tries to make sense of the complexities and anxieties of the postwar urban experience by exploring the rotten underside of the American city, the place where the American dream goes to die.

It makes sense that many of these films would be shot in L.A., close to the movie studios, and in New York, the country's largest and most iconographic city. But what explains the preponderance of films shot in San Francisco? Only the twelfth largest American city in the 1940 national census, San Francisco was remote enough in the movie-going public's consciousness that the openings of many of the films set there in this period feel it necessary to begin with a civic primer. "San Francisco: one of America's twelve great cities," boasts the narrator at the beginning of *Chinatown at Midnight*, perhaps hoping the message might resonate with viewers in some of the other top twelve cities, like Baltimore or Pittsburgh. "This is my town: San Francisco," says William Bendix at the beginning of *Race Street*, as we're shown a series of shots of downtown. *City on a Hunt* begins with an introduction by a voice that sounds as if it belongs to some kind of deranged tour guide: "This is San Francisco. This is the Golden Gate Bridge. This is the Bay Bridge. Whether you live in a mansion on Nob Hill or in an old alley in Chinatown, you'll be happy just to be in San Francisco." *The Maltese Falcon*, *Shadow of a Woman*, and *Nora Prentiss* open with the words "San Francisco" superimposed over stock footage of the city's landmarks, just in case the sight of the Golden Gate Bridge or the Ferry Building might fail to arouse in the viewer a glimmer of recognition.

Undoubtedly San Francisco's proximity to L.A. was appealing to film-makers, but this does not begin to explain the proliferation of film noirs shot in the city (after all, how many San Diego noirs can you recall?). The city's labyrinthine and at times claustrophobic architecture and its rollercoaster topography supplied cinematographers with all the severe camera angles they could have ever hoped for. Think of Joan Crawford's heels rapping down a steep, fog-slicked slope in Russian Hill at the end of *Sudden Fear*; the rooftop chase at the beginning of *Vertigo*, when the city drops away like an abyss under the dangling Jimmy Stewart; the dark alleyway chase scenes in *Chinatown at Midnight*; the man flung off of a Chinatown fire escape in *Woman on the Run*; the chase up the endless Filbert Steps in *Treasure of Monte Cristo*; the mysterious hole in the back wall of a garage that gives way to a steep drop off a cliff at the top of Telegraph Hill, in *The House on Telegraph Hill*; and the list goes on. In case the reader hasn't seen any of these films, I should say simply that the inclines are steep, the drops long, the alleys narrow, the light from the streetlamps spectral, and the camera angles nosebleed. The few wide-open spaces have a lifeless, post-apocalyptic quality. They are often urban ruins, like the abandoned military base Fort Point (*The Man Who*

Cheated Himself, Point Blank) and Alcatraz Island, after the prison had closed down (*Point Blank* again); or they are familiar public spaces like Candlestick Park (*Experiment in Terror*) and the ice skating rink at Sutro's Baths (*The Lineup*), where the crowds go about with their petty pleasures, pathetically ignorant of the murderers among them. In San Francisco one never knows what's lurking just over the crest of the next hill or in the dark recesses of the nearest alley. In the movies, at least, it's usually something holding a large revolver.

Filmmakers were also drawn to San Francisco's peculiar mythology, its reputation as a city of misfits and double-crossers. This reputation dates back to the gold-rush era, when the city was nicknamed, with a mixture of derision and terror, the "Barbary Coast," for its loose morals and looser rule of law. A number of early films, such as *San Francisco* and *Barbary Coast*, pay tribute to this lawless time, but only in a lighthearted, mawkish way. In the San Francisco of film noir, violence and vice thrive as never before, but in a different form. Criminal activity is sublimated, hidden from the view of respectable citizens, seething just below the surface of this glamorous, glossy city.

From the Gold Rush to the Silicon Rush, San Francisco has come to represent an American El Dorado, beckoning speculators and gamblers, men who come to the city to reverse their fortunes and reinvent themselves, only to fail miserably in the end—another theme central to film noir. *Nora Prentiss* takes this formula to manic proportions: respectable family man and medical practitioner Richard Talbot (Kent Smith) becomes obsessed by lust for nightclub singer Nora Prentiss (Ann Sheridan). He begins to spend his nights at the nightclub and his weekends on spontaneous excursions with his young girlfriend. Finally he gives up his old life altogether, pushing his old self off a cliff, literally (that is, he fakes his own death). He leaves town, has plastic surgery, and returns to the city as a new man with a new name, Richard Thompson. But as soon as he's returned to San Francisco, as Richard Thompson, he is charged with the murder of Richard Talbot. At the trial his own wife is unable to recognize him. He receives the death sentence.

As much as the films in this collection evoke a sense of a noir San Francisco, they also provide a cross section of the larger trends in film noir, as it has evolved in the years since *The Maltese Falcon* (1941). The film noirs of the early 1940s were often inspired by hardboiled detective fiction written by authors like Hammett, Raymond Chandler, James M. Cain, and Cornell Woolrich. The chilling *This Gun for Hire* (1942), for instance, which is set in San Francisco but was not shot there, was adapted from a story by Graham Greene. The end of the war brought about darker, highly cynical films like *Born to Kill* (1947), starring Lawrence Tierney as one of the most irredeemably evil characters in all of film noir, and *Out of the Past* (1947), *D.O.A.* (1950), and *The Man Who Cheated Himself* (1950), films whose tragic conclusions are foreseeable from their very first scenes. At the same time there emerged a series of films inspired in part by documentary filmmaking during the war and Italian neorealism's flat, deliberate style. A new kind of noir, the police procedural, became increasingly prominent. In films like *Chinatown at Midnight* (1949), the viewer is guided through a meticulous, and often tedious, homicide investigation. The Red Scare inspired politically-edged films like the subtle socialistic allegory, *Thieves' Highway* (1949), the film that led to director Jules Dassin being blacklisted, and, at the other extreme, *I Married a Communist* (1950), with its grim character assassination of San Francisco labor leader Harry Bridges.

The period of classic film noir reached its culmination with psychologically introspective films like *The Lady from Shanghai* (1948), *Woman on the Run* (1950), and *The House on Telegraph Hill* (1951). These films are distinguished by aloof characters with inscrutable motives, who are haunted by personal demons and lack anything resembling moral conviction. *The Sniper* (1952), one of the first films about a serial killer (now a genre unto itself), is an extreme case. The hero is a psychopath, yet we are made to sympathize with his profound alienation from society when we learn about his mother's cruelty and when we witness the antipathy of doctors and policemen, too callous and entangled in bureaucracy to respond to his desperate pleas for help—at least until it's too late. Subversively, the film's other characters are so obnoxious and unfeeling that the psychotic killer often seems humane in contrast.

Touch of Evil (April 23, 1958) is widely considered to be the last classic film noir by critics who cite Orson Welles' hyperbolic manipulation of standard noir conventions; it was the brawniest, most self-conscious noir yet. After this film, noir entered a period of hibernation or ended altogether, depending on the critic. I would argue that it entered a fallow period that lasted nearly three whole weeks, until May 9, 1958, when Alfred Hitchcock's *Vertigo* was released, marking the beginning of the neo-noir era. *Vertigo* has much in common with earlier noirs, beginning with the plot: a private investigator is led into a nebulous mystery by a beguiling femme fatale, with whom he soon falls in love. The film revisits familiar noir motifs, such as the innocent man assailed by vast, conspiratorial forces; the psychologically unstable, or neurotic, anti-hero; the effete, over-intellectualized criminal mastermind; and the faked death. Structurally Hitchcock uses repetition, or doubling, to give the viewer a feeling of being caught in a labyrinth that always turns back on itself, with no way out. The tragedy that impels the film's mystery— Carlotta Valdes' suicide—is, like a bad nightmare, destined to repeat itself over and over again, despite our hero's fraught efforts.

Yet *Vertigo* does break with the classic noir tradition, and the break is profound. By the late 1950s, noir was in danger of collapsing under the weight of its own time-wearied conventions. Hitchcock revitalized noir by turning upside down its most identifiable characteristics. In *Vertigo* he traded black and white film for color, tough-guy argot for naturalistic dialogue, and a hard-edged realism for a fantastical, otherworldly feel. In the first half of the film, it's unclear whether we are watching a detective story or a ghost story. Yet the result is a film that is as paranoid as *Crisscross*, as suspenseful as *The Big Sleep*, as bitterly disillusioned as *Double Indemnity*, as haunting as *Laura*, and more breathtakingly beautiful than all of them.

A dull nostalgia for the bygone era nevertheless persisted in the following years, yielding films like *Portrait in Black* (1960), which veers precipitously toward domestic melodrama, and *Experiment in Terror* (1962), which comes closer to satire. *Point Blank* (1967), however, ushered in a new series of films by directors that had been avid fans of noir in their youth. These filmmakers did not attempt to replicate the whole noir formula but instead amplified a single noir theme or motif to a nearly obsessive degree, creating films that shared noir's genetic code but had mutated beyond recognition. *Point Blank*, for instance, seems to tell the familiar story of a professional killer in vengeful pursuit of a man who stole his loot and his wife, and tried to murder him. But Walker (Lee Marvin), the killer, is so heartless and implacable that he can barely even speak or show any sign of emotion whatsoever—not even anger or relief. He is a machine; he is a ghost.

Following in the tradition of *The Big Heat* (1955), *Bullitt* (1968) and *Dirty Harry* (1971) are, at first glance, about vigilante cops who seek justice at all costs, even if that means breaking the law. But Steve McQueen's Frank Bullitt and Clint Eastwood's Harry Callahan are not driven to action by personal tragedy, like Glenn Ford's Sergeant Bannion in *The Big Heat*. Like Walker, Bullitt and Harry are distant, not-quite-human characters. They seem driven less by any kind of higher moral calling, such as retribution or justice, than by a lurid fervor for violence. *The Conversation* (1974) and *Invasion of the Body Snatchers* (1978) explore the classic noir theme of paranoia, but so obsessively that, by the end of each film, nothing else remains. In these films paranoia, left alone to fester long enough, turns into insanity.

Neo-noirs made in the last twenty years have a tendency to revert to glib exercises in nostalgia (*Hammett* [1982]) or playful, but not genuinely menacing, reworkings of familiar material (*Jagged Edge* [1985], *Final Analysis* [1992]). Some impressively innovative neo-noirs have been made during this time—*Blood Simple* (1984), *Blue Velvet* (1986), *The Usual Suspects* (1995), *Mulholland Drive* (2001) are a small sample—films that continue to challenge familiar noir formulas and create new hybrid genres in the process. Unfortunately very few of the best noirs in recent decades have been filmed in San Francisco, perhaps because the city is so closely identified with many of noir's most influential and familiar films. One exception is the underappreciated *Basic Instinct* (1992), unfairly maligned for a single famously prurient shot of Sharon Stone. Although its plot, characters, narrative structure, sets, and even costumes derive directly from *Vertigo*, director Paul Verhoeven's approach has much in common with that of the iconoclastic 1970s neo-noirs. Like those films, it focuses on a single motif, in this case Hitchcock's motif of doubling, and exaggerates it to a lunatic degree. Virtually every event in *Basic Instinct*, including murder, occurs at least twice; every character has a doppelgänger; scenes are restaged with the identical shot sequence; lines of dialogue are repeated verbatim in different contexts.

The film even has two endings. It's a novelty, something like *Vertigo* on steroids, but one that deserves a closer look nonetheless.

Vigilant noir enthusiasts will observe that this collection has omitted several San Francisco noirs. These include *This Gun for Hire* (1942), *Shadow of a Woman* (1946), *Undercurrent* (1946), *Raw Deal* (1948), *Blonde Ice* (1948), *Shakedown* (1950), *Crime of Passion* (1957) and *I Want to Live!* (1958). That is because these films omit San Francisco. Despite being set, at least partially, in the city, they feature no real shots of the city nor do they even pretend to be set in any actual San Francisco locations. They rely on flat backdrops, soundstages, and stock footage to create an ersatz San Francisco. Moreover, since film noir is no exact science, some readers will surely quarrel with the inclusion of certain films, while others will point out further omissions. A large bulk of the existing body of literature on noir has tried to provide an authoritative definition of "film noir." Some studies propose a list of characteristics that might be used as a kind of cinematic Diagnostic Statistical Manual to classify films as either noir or not noir, while other collections, usually no thinner than the white pages of Bay Area telephone directories, generate a catalogue of films that might constitute a noir canon, as if such a slippery, changeable category would readily submit to such rigid classification.

I encourage those interested in a more academic and comprehensive approach to film noir to consult, as I have, *The Film Noir Reader*, edited by Alain Silver and James Ursini, which contains several of the earliest and most famous essays written on the subject. These include Raymond Borde and Étienne Chaumeton's "Towards a Definition of Film Noir," an excerpt from *Panorama du film noir américain*; Raymond Durgnat's "Paint It Black: The Family Tree of the Film Noir" (1970), which lists eleven "dominant cycles or motifs" of film noir, including "Crime as Social Criticism," "On the Run," "Private Eyes and Adventurers," "Portraits and Doubles," and "Psychopaths"; Janey Place and Lowell Peterson's "Some Visual Motifs of Film Noir" (1974); and Paul Schrader's "Notes on Film Noir" (1972), a concise analysis of film noir's central themes and stylistic attributes. (Silver also edited, with Elizabeth Ward, the exhaustive and reliable *Film Noir: An Encyclopedic Reference to the American Style*.) Two recent, more accessible, entries are the engaging, street-smart *Dark City: The Lost World of Film Noir* by the San

Francisco-based noir expert Eddie Muller, and Nicholas Christopher's engrossing *Somewhere in the Night: Film Noir and the American City*, a book whose subject dovetails with my own.

The locations featured in this book betray film noir's predilection for unusual, forgotten urban spaces. Many are quite unremarkable in themselves: a narrow alleyway, an abandoned theater, a fenced-in house. Others are not places at all, but gaps in the urban grid, holes that these films have filled with their own warped tales. When familiar locations do appear in these films, like Ocean Beach, Alcatraz, or Union Square, they are rendered strange and menacing, almost unrecognizable. In noir San Francisco, Ocean Beach is not a fun place to go surfing but a mirage of shifting sand dunes at the edge of the world where people go to be murdered. Alcatraz is not a prison, or a tourist destination that sells its own refrigerator magnets, but an abandoned island ruin, ideal for a major drug heist. The quality of the films included here is, to put it gently, diverse. Masterpieces like *The Maltese Falcon*, *Out of the Past*, *Vertigo*, and *Point Blank* share space with fun camp (*Chinatown at Midnight*, *Pacific Heights*) and not-so-fun dreck (*Race Street*, *Final Analysis*). But each film evokes a sense of a San Francisco that is quite different from the one depicted in tour guides and romantic comedies. I hope this curious book can serve as a map for this other San Francisco, where it's always night, where the fog is thick with dread, and where no one ever dies—they only get murdered.

Nathaniel Rich
San Francisco

THE HOUSE ACROSS THE BAY:
ALCATRAZ

George Raft and Joan Bennett in *The House Across the Bay*, 1940. Photofest.

Director: Archie Mayo
Cast: Joan Bennett, George Raft, Lloyd Nolan, Walter Pidgeon
Cinematographer: Merritt B. Gerstad
Walter Wanger Productions, 1940

T he house of the film's title is not actually across the Bay, but in it: it's Alcatraz Penitentiary, the Big House itself. It's there that racketeer Steve Larwitt (the consummately humorless George Raft) lands after wife Brenda (Joan Bennett) tips off the IRS to his inventive tax calculus. But this isn't the dreary, brutal Alcatraz memorialized in later films like *Escape from Alcatraz* or *Birdman of Alcatraz*. Steve's life as an inmate is rather cozy: he wears a smart button-over jumpsuit, passes his days in the laundry detail, and jokes around with his wife when she visits, saying that he loves her so much that he might even break out of jail for her.

What Steve won't do for love he'll do for rage. After his crooked lawyer, appropriately named Slant (Lloyd Nolan), informs him that his wife is running around San Francisco with airplane manufacturer Tim Nolan (Walter Pidgeon), Steve decides to escape and give his ungrateful wife what she has coming to her. After pulling the old pillows-under-the-blanket routine to trick the guards into thinking he's asleep, Steve surfaces in the middle of the Bay. He evades the searchlights by a clever ruse: he simply ducks underwater whenever they shine his way.

After Steve exacts his revenge, he does something that is unprecedented in Alcatraz escape history: he tries to break back in. The guards, still patrolling the Bay, spot him with their searchlight. This time Steve doesn't duck under the surface in time and dies a death that is unusually gruesome for such an early film noir.

If the idea of such an easy escape from Alcatraz seems inconceivable in retrospect, it's worth noting that *The House Across the Bay* was made just three years after the attempted escape of inmates Theodore Cole and Ralph Roe. The two friends had been transferred from Leavenworth two years earlier; Cole was serving fifty years for kidnapping and Roe ninety-nine years for armed robbery. They chose the prison's Model Industries Building as their getaway spot. This building, which sits at the island's western tip, was well-known among prisoners to be the one place on Alcatraz hidden from the view of the guards posted in the prison's watchtowers. During an unsupervised session in the mat shop on December 16, 1937, Cole and Roe sawed through the heavy glass panes and iron bars of the shop's window, carving a hole that was just eight and three-quarter inches high by eighteen inches long. They climbed over a wire fence and dropped fifteen feet to a narrow rocky beach, never to be seen again.

Guards found no trace of the men in a search of the surrounding waters, which was not entirely surprising, since that day the Bay was experiencing one of the densest fogs in recorded history. When the F.B.I. finally closed its investigation into Cole and Roe's disappearance thirty years later, it released a report concluding that the men had drowned in the Bay's powerful undertow, which is known to suck swimmers down by their feet. The tide would have dragged their bodies out to sea, which would explain the authorities' inability to locate the corpses.

There are other theories, however. In the years following the escape, the *San Francisco Chronicle* repeatedly reported various sightings of the men: shortly after the escape, two suspicious men stole food from campers in the Muir Woods; a year and a half after the escape, several old acquaintances of Roe claimed to have spotted him in the vicinity of his hometown, Shawnee, Oklahoma; around the same time, a man arrested for murder said he had played poker with the two men in Pueblo, Colorado; in April 1940, a pair of hitchhikers reported being picked up by the two men in Tulsa; and the next day, still in Tulsa, a critically wounded taxicab driver told the local police that he had seen the two men, and had been shot by Cole when he had recognized them from their mug shots in the newspaper.

Finally, in 1941, the *Chronicle* ran a front-page article claiming that the missing men were alive and living like princes in South America.

Cole and Roe had told two inmate friends that if their escape succeeded, they would send a letter with a code phrase indicating that they were safe. The letter arrived in July of 1938, bearing the secret code "business was good in July." Based on information revealed by undisclosed sources, the article went on to piece together the details of the escape. In the fog a third man had left two oil barrels on the Alcatraz beach, one of which contained civilian clothes, to be used as a getaway raft. The strong current—for it was high tide—swept them out beyond the Golden Gate Bridge to the shores of Marin County. After sneaking south they passed across the border and were smuggled from a Mexican port to Central America. The *Chronicle* reporter cheerily concluded that Cole and Roe "have resided for periods in both Peru and Chile...are reported to have plenty of money today, [and are] living comfortably in their South American hideouts."

THE MALTESE FALCON:
BURRITT ALLEY

Ward Bond and Humphrey Bogart in *The Maltese Falcon*, 1941. Photofest.

Director: John Huston
Cast: Humphrey Bogart, Mary Astor, Peter Lorre, Sydney Greenstreet
Cinematographer: Arthur Edeson
First National Pictures Inc./Warner Bros., 1941

BURRITT ALLEY
Off of Bush Street, between the Stockton Street Tunnel and Dashiell Hammett Street
DON HERRON'S DASHIELL HAMMETT TOUR
Given on select Sundays
See www.donherron.com for details

The Maltese Falcon is not only the most widely admired San Francisco film noir, but it is the one most readily associated with the city. This is because, in part, director John Huston gives extraordinary, even obsessive, attention to the city's geography. When the film begins, the first words on the screen are not the title of the film, but "San Francisco," in large white letters superimposed over a shot of the Golden Gate Bridge. And not only does Huston constantly remind us what city we're in, but he gives us our exact coordinates within it at all times. Just as in Dashiell Hammett's novel, the film charts Sam Spade's interminable divagations around San Francisco with bizarre accuracy, overwhelming the viewer with street signs and addresses. These include, but are not limited to: 111 Sutter Street at Montgomery; 416 Post Street; 26 Burlingame, 12C; the Carpenter Apartments on 1001 California Street; the intersection of Geary and Leavenworth; The Bailey Theater; The Florence Hotel; the St. Mark Hotel; the St. Francis Hotel; the Hotel Belvedere, Room 635; the Embarcadero; the Ferry Building; the Golden Gate Bridge; the Bay Bridge; and, of course, Burritt Alley, by the intersection of Bush and Stockton, where Brigid O'Shaughnessy guns down Spade's partner Miles Archer. The torrent of numbers and locations does more than simply serve as a constant reminder of the presence of the city in the film. More importantly, they function to overwhelm the viewer with meaningless details, just as Sam Spade, in his search for the Maltese Falcon, finds himself lost in a baroque tangle of contradicting and puzzling information. Huston forces us to share in Spade's confusion, as we vainly try to register all this information and ascribe some kind of logic to it. Like Spade, we're bound to fail.

Yet just as Spade encounters red-herrings and blind alleys, the many shots of street signs and room numbers are themselves misleading. *The Maltese Falcon* was not actually shot in San Francisco. Most of the scenes are interior shots, filmed at the Warner Bros. Studio in Burbank, California. In several instances, Huston uses stock footage for the establishing shots of the city. If you look closely at the shot of the Ferry Building in the opening scene, you can see a sign reading "Golden Gate Bridge … Fiesta May 27." This sign advertised a celebration for the opening of the bridge—in 1937, four years before the film's actual production. Worse, in a scene meant to take place on a pier on the Embarcadero, a group of firefighters wear LAFD helmets.

Today a bronze plaque marks the real Burritt Alley, commemorating the site of Archer's demise. Although Spade fans discussed the idea of a memorial in the early sixties after the deaths of Bogart (1957) and Hammett (1961), the plaque did not go up until 1974, after the kind of wrangling and confusion that one finds in a Hammett novel. The details of the story behind the plaque, along with most other details about Hammett's literature and life, are the subjects of a walking tour given by the writer Don Herron, a leading expert on Hammett. His four-hour and three-mile Dashiell Hammett tour is currently in its twenty-eighth year, making it the longest-running literary tour of its kind. Although Herron used to give the tour every Sunday, he now runs a more restricted schedule, hoping to limit the tour to serious Hammett fans; he happily discourages curious tourists from attending. "It's not," he warns, "like going to Alcatraz." For those dedicated to Hammett, however, Herron is the perfect guide, with his trenchcoat and brown fedora, and a low gravelly voice that tells it straight down the line every time. In fact Dashiell Hammett gives a fairly accurate description of Herron's countenance in the first paragraph of *The Maltese Falcon*, when he writes that his "jaw was long and bony, his chin a jutting v under the more flexible v of his mouth…."

NORA PRENTISS:
DINARDO'S

Ann Sheridan in *Nora Prentiss*, 1947. Photofest.

Director: Vincent Sherman
Cast: Ann Sheridan, Kent Smith, Robert Alda, Bruce Bennett
Cinematographer: James Wong Howe
Warner Bros., 1947

LOU'S PIER 47 RESTAURANT AND BLUES CLUB
300 Jefferson Street
Sunday–Friday: 4 pm–12 am; Saturday: 12 pm–1 am
☎ (415) 771-LOUS
POMPEI'S GROTTO
340 Jefferson Street
Daily 8 am–11 pm
☎ (415) 776-9265

D r. Richard Talbot (Kent Smith), a humdrum family physician, experiences a rare thrill when he is called to treat a nightclub singer who has been sideswiped by a taxicab on the street outside his office. He grudgingly takes a liking to the woman, who introduces herself as Nora Prentiss (the gorgeous, if falconiform, Ann Sheridan). A fine physical specimen indeed, thinks Talbot, and before long he is imagining himself doing all kinds of crazy things to win her fancy. As the trailer to the film puts it: "She's the kind of woman that happens to a man once— once too often!"

Plagued by untoward thoughts, and with his wife conveniently out of town, he decides to spend an evening at the nightclub—spurred only by curiosity, he tells himself. Respectable people go to nightclubs too, don't they? He puts aside a paper on which he's hard at work (on "the ailments of the heart"), and heads toward Dinardo's nightclub at Fisherman's Wharf. While he watches Nora sing "Would You Like A Souvenir?" his mustache furrows with lascivious merriment; when she approaches his table, mid-act, singing the line "If your conscience hurts, don't let it / Come and get it while it's here," he suffers from his own ailment of the heart.

The nightclub's interior was not shot on location, but we are given a rare nighttime view of 1940s Fisherman's Wharf. Talbot passes the fishing boats docked off of Pier 45, near Jones Street, and the crab stands along Jefferson Street, before reaching a poster of Nora Prentiss outside

Dinardo's. Today another jazz club stands there: Lou's Pier 47. Although it lacks the fictional nightclub's checkered tablecloths, art-deco table lamps, and (most glaringly) Ann Sheridan, Lou's Pier 47 is a respectable ribs-and-jazz joint. To get a glimpse of the real 1940s Fisherman's Wharf, go next door to Pompei's Grotto, which opened in 1946—the year *Nora Prentiss* was filmed—and has barely changed since. There you'll find the old wood-paneled bar, the wicker wine baskets containing jugs of Chianti, and a fat plate of Crab Cioppino, a specialty of the original owner's mother, Lucia, who came to San Francisco from the Italian fishing village of San Benedetto d'Ancona. Instead of Adriatic crabs, the crabs are now Dungeness, fresh out of the Bay.

Nora Prentiss is, in one sense at least, a noir in reverse. In many noirs, a righteous hero is led into a confusing labyrinth by a mysterious, beguiling woman. In *Nora Prentiss*, the evil plotter is not the charming Nora Prentiss but Talbot himself. He creates his own labyrinth and brings about his own ruin. Desperate to leave his wife for Nora, but unable to bear a divorce, he decides instead to stage his own murder. When he torches his old identity and sends it careening over a cliff into the Bay, he becomes a new man with a new name: Richard Thompson. He escapes to New York with Nora, who manages somehow to remain aloof, oblivious of his bizarre machinations and the extent of his deceit until it's too late. Despite her acid tongue and her job as a nightclub singer, Nora turns out to be as wholesome as Lucia's Crab Cioppino.

Talbot's plodding, systematic descent into madness makes *Nora Prentiss* a more sinister noir than the film's staid early scenes would seem to promise. The sequence where Talbot grows delusional and claustrophobic while secluded in a New York hotel room is particularly distressing, and can be seen as a model for the final scene of *The Conversation* (1974), in which surveillance expert Harry Caul dismantles his room in the throes of a violent attack of paranoia. Like that later film, *Nora Prentiss* ends with its virtuous hero manic and bent on self-destruction. When, disguised as Thompson, Talbot is charged for his own murder, he accepts the court's guilty verdict with an eerie sense of relief.

BORN TO KILL:
OCEAN BEACH

Lawrence Tierney and Elisha Cook, Jr., in *Born to Kill*, 1947. Photofest.

Director: Robert Wise
Cast: Claire Trevor, Lawrence Tierney, Elisha Cook, Jr.
Cinematographer: Robert De Grasse
RKO, 1947

OCEAN BEACH
The Pacific coast off the Great Highway

B *orn to Kill* opens in a dazzlingly bright city putrid with sin. There's boozing, gambling, easy sex, a beer-guzzling hag, a two-timing chippy, a depraved thug, his scheming toady, and a gold-digging divorcee, and to top it off, two brutal murders and a midnight getaway. Then things really get out of hand. They leave Reno and go to San Francisco.

Sam Wilde (Lawrence Tierney) is a monster, one of the most brutal killers in all of film noir, ranking right up there with sadists like *The Big Heat*'s Vince Stone (Lee Marvin) and *The Glass Key*'s Jeff (William Bendix). Unlike them, however, Tierney gets top billing. He's no henchman and he won't settle for second fiddle. As he says, he'll kill "anytime I see anyone making a monkey out of me." He means it, and his definition of "monkey" is rather broad.

Sam does not figure in the film's meanest, and most memorable, scene, however—at least not at first. Sam's devoted lackey Marty Waterman (Elisha Cook, Jr.) lures the blustery old Mrs. Kraft (Esther Howard) to meet him in the sand dunes at the edge of the city. Mrs. Kraft is desperate to find out who killed her young friend Laury Palmer (a quest that will resonate for fans of a certain neo-noir television series). Marty, by claiming he has information about the killer's identity, entices Mrs. Kraft to meet him at Ocean Beach.

She hobbles out of a cab at a desolate crossroads in the middle of the night. The cabbie, despite his misgivings at leaving the old woman stranded far from the nearest bus station or cabstand, finally pulls away, leaving her alone in the light of a single streetlamp. The beach is not visible but the glow of the streetlamp picks out clouds of sand skipping off the nearby dunes. All of a sudden a man's hand reaches out of the shadows and taps her on the shoulder. She turns to see Marty's horrible grinning face. He leads her past the end of the road and up to a twinned crest in the dunes. As the sand continues to gust across the screen, with no water in sight, it seems as if this mismatched pair has stumbled upon a desert, ghostly and without end, at the edge of the world. Marty helps Mrs. Kraft over the bluff. Once they're out of sight, Marty pulls a shiv; Mrs. Kraft headbutts him and takes off, somehow eluding his reach, and tumbles down the bluff toward the road. Just as Marty is about to close in, a hulking figure runs out of the darkness behind him. It's Sam, eager to show Marty what real cruelty is.

Ocean Beach is the wide strand of beach that separates the city from the Pacific Ocean. Although it's not as picturesque or as secluded as Baker or China Beach, it's the most popular beach in San Francisco. This is due, in part, to the large breakers, which make for the city's best surfing. It's also the only city beach on which it is permitted to light a bonfire. A killer like Marty would never lure an unsuspecting victim there today, since the beach is no longer a dark, secluded location, but a popular alternative to the city's nightlife (although the occasional waterlogged body does wash to shore from time to time).

DARK PASSAGE:
THE MALLOCH
APARTMENT BUILDING

Lauren Bacall and Humphrey Bogart in *Dark Passage*, 1947. Photofest.

Director: Delmer Daves
Cast: Humphrey Bogart, Lauren Bacall, Agnes Moorehead
Cinematographer: Sid Hickox
Warner Bros., 1947

THE MALLOCH APARTMENT BUILDING
1360 Montgomery Street, between Alta and Filbert Streets

D eluding cosmetic surgery hopefuls for nearly sixty years now, *Dark Passage* is the third and strangest of the four films that Humphrey Bogart and Lauren Bacall made together. It is also among the first in a small group of films to use transformative plastic surgery as a central plot device (the best of which are John Woo's *Face/Off*, Bruce Lee's *Game of Death*, and the "Eye of the Beholder" episode of the *Twilight Zone*). But once the plot unravels into absurdity, it is Bogart and Bacall's tender relationship that carries this film noir oddity.

Vincent Parry, who has been wrongly convicted of murdering his wife, makes a clean sneak from San Quentin. Fortunately for him he is picked up on the highway by the sympathetic landscape artist Irene Jansen (Lauren Bacall). Vincent, whose face we don't see for the first third of the film, has plastic surgery in order to avoid being recognized by the authorities. When he finally removes his bandages, and we see him for the first time, he has morphed into…Humphrey Bogart. Irene could not be more pleased. As Vincent grows increasingly paranoid about being detected (and as the plot grows increasingly far-fetched), director Delmer Daves tightens the city's geography accordingly. The city's steep hills and shrouded passages collapse into a sinister labyrinth that forces Vincent into chance encounters with all the people he is running from— the cops, a blackmailer who knows his identity, and worst of all, Madge Rapf (Agnes Moorehead), the shrewish friend of his murdered wife.

The film's deepening sense of claustrophobia is felt nowhere more strongly than in Irene's apartment in the Malloch Apartment Building. Vincent uses the apartment as his hideout while he tries to find his wife's real murderer. Peeking through one of the Malloch's signature plate glass windows, he spots Madge staring at him from across the street; coming out of the shower he hears Madge knocking at the door. He can't even fumble through Irene's personal belongings without Irene walking in on him. Riddled and desperate, Vincent can think of no escape but to enter the maze of downtown San Francisco, thus beginning the string of deadly encounters that drives the second half of the film.

The Malloch Apartment Building was designed in the Streamline Moderne style in 1937 by Irvin Goldstine and Jack S. and J. Rolph Malloch, a father-and-son contracting team who were its first residents. The four-story, white-and-silver building stands just a block south of the edge of Telegraph Hill, right after Montgomery Street splits into two levels, and is sheltered by English hawthorne trees, giant dracaena, and a bright shrub of pink geraniums. Two forty-foot-high *sgraffito* murals by Alfred du Pont cover its north and west walls. One mural depicts Commerce, a strong, barrel-chested figure who cradles the earth in his arms. In the background a freighter passes beneath the Bay Bridge, which was completed in the same year as the Malloch. From the other mural gazes bright-eyed Discovery, at whose feet sit a compass and a gold-rush-era clipper. The building's most remarkable feature, however, is the elevator that Bogart rides in *Dark Passage*. It can be accessed through a silver reflective door located in the lobby atrium. The frosted glass elevator shaft is exposed to the street and is backlit, so that you can see the elevator cage rising at night, as if through liquid silver.

The current resident of Irene's third-floor apartment has posted in her window a cardboard cutout of Bogart. He smokes a cigarette and appears to be sizing up Coit Tower, which looms just ahead of him, across Montgomery. He stands on permanent watch for any intruders or, even worse, the ghost of Madge Rapf.

OUT OF THE PAST:
ERSATZ SAN FRANCISCO

Virginia Huston and Robert Mitchum in *Out of the Past*, 1947. Photofest.

Director: Jacques Tourneur
Cast: Robert Mitchum, Jane Greer, Kirk Douglas, Virginia Huston
Cinematographer: Nicholas Musuraca
RKO, 1947

Rarely do movie stars have any difficulty faking a tear or a temper tantrum. But few can convincingly act humble. As *Out of the Past*'s Kirk Douglas said, "Making movies is a form of narcissism." Robert Mitchum is the exception: he was so skilled at self-deprecation that he convinced several generations of film critics (another group not particularly inclined to humility) that he was a bad actor. His sleep-walk and his famously inert face—his eyes peering out as if from behind a mold of aspic—was readily misconstrued as a blank acting style. His colleagues often agreed with the critics. On the set of *Undercurrent*, Katharine Hepburn, who barely shared any screen time with him, gave it to him straight. "You can't act," she said, "and if you hadn't been good-looking you would never have gotten the picture." As Mitchum himself put it: "Listen. I got three expressions: looking left, looking right, and looking straight ahead."

In *Out of the Past*, he has one of his greatest roles as Jeff Bailey, a man who, like Mitchum himself, is underestimated by his foes because of his dull, indolent demeanor. Millionaire Whit Sterling (Douglas) and his inscrutable girlfriend Kathie Moffat (Jane Greer) draw Jeff into their nebulous world of tax evasion, theft, blackmail, and murder, taking him for a chump. What they don't realize is that no chump talks this smoothly. Take, for instance, this exchange:

KATHIE: Don't Jeff.

JEFF: Don't what?

KATHIE: I don't want to die.

JEFF: Neither do I baby, but if I have to, I'm going to die last.

or:

KATHIE: I had to come back. What else could I do?

JEFF: You can never help anything, can you? You're like a leaf that the wind blows from one gutter to another.

After *The Maltese Falcon*, *Out of the Past* is the most famous of the classic San Francisco noirs, despite the fact that, like that earlier film, virtually none of it was actually shot in the city. The movie theater in North Beach, the Mason Building (Leonard Eels' office), 114 Fulton Street (Eels' apartment), Teeter's restaurant, the Sterling Club, and the Telegraph Hill apartment of Meta Carson, Eels' secretary, are all invented locations (114 Fulton Street would be somewhere in the middle of the Civic Center). This makes a certain amount of poetic sense given that Jeff's long treasure hunt through the San Francisco night is a charade, carefully rigged to frame him for the crimes that his employer has committed along the way. Even the place and character names betray the illusory, ersatz nature of Jeff's nightmarish adventure. The characters are slippery ("Eels") and ever-changing ("Meta"); his fate hangs precariously in the balance ("Teeter's") as his quest to figure out who is setting him up, and for what crimes, leads him to The Mason Building, where his investigation attains an even murkier (Masonic) level of intrigue. Our creeping suspicion that we are not in San Francisco but in a clapboard model of the city only echoes Jeff's growing conviction that he's being framed; that the people he meets are actors; and that their apartments are sets which have been meticulously designed to trick him into taking the fall for Whit Sterling's criminal enterprises. The locations seem to have been constructed only to provide director Jacques Tourneur with a wealth of dark hallways, blind alleys, steep staircases, and empty rooms. This dummy San Francisco coheres into a labyrinth out of which Jeff, despite his smooth talk and clever stealth, cannot escape.

THE LADY FROM SHANGHAI:
STEINHART AQUARIUM

Orson Welles and Rita Hayworth in *The Lady from Shanghai*, 1948. Photofest.

Director: Orson Welles
Cast: Orson Welles, Rita Hayworth, Everett Sloane
Cinematographer: Charles Lawton, Jr.
Columbia Pictures, 1948

STEINHART AQUARIUM
875 Howard Street
Open daily 10 am–5 pm
☎ (415) 321-8000

B y the time production began on *The Lady from Shanghai*, Orson
Welles' marriage to Rita Hayworth had all but disintegrated. Although
they had not yet filed for divorce, Hayworth was shacked up with the
romantic balladeer Tony Martin, while Welles had "discovered" the
French ingénue Barbara Laage. Their lawyers were in the midst of argu-
ing over the details of a property settlement. Nevertheless, Welles badly
needed his wife's star power to convince Columbia Pictures to give his
film a large budget. As was the case so often throughout his career,
Welles himself was nearly broke and needed a winner so that he could
finance future film projects. Hayworth, a steadfast admirer of her husband's work, committed to the project well in advance, despite their fail-
ing relationship.

   Disaster plagued the film's production from the very beginning.
Welles ordered Hayworth to chop off her famous red locks and dye her
cropped hair platinum blond, traumatizing both her and Harry Cohn, the
head of Columbia, in an incident that the press would call "The Million
Dollar Haircut." The shoot began off the shore of Acapulco, aboard Errol
Flynn's yacht, the *Zaca* (Flynn plays the ship's skipper in the film). On
the first day a camera assistant collapsed dead from a heart attack.
Flynn, serially drunk, and frightened that the death would attract undue
attention to the nightly debauches he staged aboard his boat, ordered the
body to be sewn inside a duffel bag and dropped in the ocean (cooler
minds prevailed and someone quietly rowed the body ashore). Soon

thereafter Hayworth fell ill from sinus problems and sunstroke, forcing delays in the shoot. Meanwhile a tropical insect stung Welles, causing his eye to swell to three times its size. He bellowed like a wounded bear all night, certain he would die. As the sweltering shoot dragged on, tempers withered further. After the last day of filming, Hayworth filed for divorce.

The film's script was a cryptic, chaotic mess, and it was rendered virtually incomprehensible when Columbia decided to abridge Welles' original two-and-a-half-hour version by a full hour. As it stands, the basic plot is as follows: Michael O'Hara (Welles), an Irish seaman, is hired by the powerful but physically crippled trial lawyer Floyd Bannister (the shrill and devilish Everett Sloane) to captain a yacht trip he is taking with his law partner, George Grisby (Glenn Anders) and Bannister's bombshell wife, Elsa (Hayworth). In Mexico, Grisby offers Mike $5,000 to help him fake his own death. Mike warily accepts, since he plans on running away with Elsa and needs the cash. When Grisby actually does turn up dead, Mike is arrested and must figure out who double-crossed him.

It's tempting to point to the film's later scenes as on-screen evidence of Welles' vilification of Hayworth, especially the famous sequence at the Hall of Mirrors in San Francisco's Whitney's Playland (long since demolished). Mike abandons the dying Elsa Bannister, effectively killing her, in a moment considered by many to be the fulfillment of Welles' misogynist, vengeful fantasies for his soon-to-be ex-wife. But a more fascinating scene, because of its surprising juxtaposition of affection and contempt, is the couple's rendezvous at the Steinhart Aquarium, just after the *Zaca* arrives in San Francisco. In the dark aquarium, as patterns of underwater light flicker across their faces, Mike and Elsa declare their love for each other and embrace, kissing for the first (and last) time. Yet even in this, the film's most tender moment, Welles reminds us in no subtle way of Elsa's sinister intent. The camera moves from the kissing couple to the tanks behind them, where a parade of piscine grotesqueries float by: a Paleozoic sea turtle, groupers the size of hippos, and a fat, writhing octopus, each beast more monstrous than the last. Mercifully a group of giggling schoolchildren jolts the couple from their creepy embrace.

The original Steinhart Aquarium was located in Golden Gate Park, but it is currently undergoing a comprehensive renovation that will not be completed until 2008. In 2004, however, the aquarium re-opened in a temporary home at 875 Howard Street. Perhaps influenced by repeated viewings of *The Lady from Shanghai*, the aquarium's designers have made sure to give their sea creatures larger spaces to swim around in: one highlight of the new space is a two-story, 20,000-gallon coral reef tank. No longer will the tanks magnify the fish to gargantuan proportions, a development that should be a comfort to schoolchildren and trysting lovers alike.

RACE STREET:
THE GOLDEN GATE THEATER

George Raft and Gale Robbins in *Race Street*, 1948. Photofest.

Director: Edward L. Marin
Cast: George Raft, William Bendix, Marilyn Maxwell
Cinematographer: J. Roy Hunt
RKO, 1948

THE GOLDEN GATE THEATER
1 Taylor Street at Golden Gate Street, off Market Street

On March 26, 1922, elite members of San Francisco high society, dressed in top hats and formal gowns, stood in a line that snaked down Taylor Street and around the block. They came to attend the opening of the much-ballyhooed Golden Gate Theater. Passing under the theater's sparkling glass-and-metal marquee they reached the box office, which frantically distributed red tickets to forty theatergoers every minute. Attendants wearing powder-blue suits and white gloves ushered the guests through the octagonal lobby, under an ornate, fan-vaulted ceiling, and up a wide white marble stairway lined with baskets of jonquils and acacia. At the top of the stairs they saw for the first time the opulent, cavernous auditorium, with its gilded proscenium and crimson velvet curtains, lit from below by two gaslights at either end of the stage. Directly above them was the auditorium's most celebrated feature, a colossal pale blue dome. One journalist attending opening night wrote in the next day's *San Francisco Chronicle* that it was "like sitting under a bit of blue sky."

After the 3,500 audience members joined to sing the national anthem, the performance began, a mixture of vaudeville and film that reached its culmination with the feature film *Too Much Wife*, "a married life comedy" starring Wanda Hawley and T. Roy Barnes. For the next thirty years the Golden Gate would continue to run these kinds of mixed bills, featuring films and shorts in addition to vaudeville and musical acts. Performers such as the Three Stooges, Bob Hope, Jack Benny, the

Marx Brothers, Ronald Reagan, George Burns, Frank Sinatra, Nat King Cole, Sammy Davis Jr., Carmen Miranda, and Louis Armstrong would appear at the Golden Gate during this period.

Race Street, a forgettable film noir starring William Bendix and the expressionless, lizard-faced George Raft, has one remarkable scene at the Golden Gate, filmed when the theater had just begun its long decline. Dan Gannin (George Raft) is a successful bookie who, for the love of a woman, decides to go legit. Just as he does so, however, he's pulled back into the scrum when a childhood friend gets zotzed by a group of East Coast mobsters trying to expand their operation out West. In his quest to find his pal's murderers, Gannin is joined by an unlikely ally, Lieutenant Barney Runson (Bendix), who's also trying to close in on these shadowy mobsters. At one point Runson takes Gannin to the Golden Gate to follow up on a hunch. Outside the theater Runson waxes poetic. "Well, here's the good old Golden Gate," he says. "Ah, there's nothing like vaudeville. You know, vaudeville's real life people—that's why I like it. A lot of acts have played this place. I guess this is one of the few vaudeville houses left." Inside, however, the theater is showing a film, not a vaudeville act; judging by the posters it's *The Bachelor and the Bobby-Soxer* (1947), starring Cary Grant, Shirley Temple, and Rudy Vallee (who had once performed on stage at the Golden Gate). Six years later, in 1954, the Golden Gate would discontinue its stage shows altogether, becoming a full-time movie palace. One might ask, as a visibly irritated Gannin does, what inspires detective Runson to launch into such an impassioned soliloquy at the sight of the old theater. There's a simple enough answer: the film's production company, RKO, owned the theater at the time. In fact, at the beginning of this scene, we see the theater's new name, written in large lights across the marquee: the RKO Golden Gate.

Over the next twenty years RKO allowed the theater to deteriorate slowly. Its seats and carpeting became tattered, and its walls' glorious polychromatic tinting dulled. Ill-advised renovations further desecrated the theater: fake walls were erected, dividing the lobby; an escalator was added next to the grand marble staircase, which was subsequently covered with carpet; and most egregiously, a second movie screen was built on the balcony, awkwardly splitting the auditorium into two theaters, at great financial cost. In 1972 RKO closed the theater, padlocked it, and left it to rot.

The theater stayed dormant for seven years before the Nederlander Organization purchased it and began a full-scale renovation. Crumpled copies of architect G. Albert Lansburgh's original blueprints were found scattered throughout the building, stuffed behind the terra cotta walls, lying in puddles on the floor of the orchestra pit, lining garbage cans in the basement, and buried under piles of trash in the attic. These plans, together with what historical photographs existed, became the basis for the vast restoration. The theater re-opened on December 27, 1979, with a performance by the touring company of *A Chorus Line*.

Today the Golden Gate remains a popular venue for Broadway national tours. Although the house is not usually open for public viewing on the day of a performance, one can still walk in and see the lobby's famous pink-and-crimson fan-vaulted ceiling and its sloped marble floor and imagine the surprised delight of its first visitors, doffing their top hats and waving their red tickets.

WALK A CROOKED MILE:
THE COMMUNIST SAFEHOUSE

Louis Hayward and Dennis O'Keefe in *Walk a Crooked Mile*, 1948. Photofest.

Director: Gordon Douglas
Cast: Dennis O'Keefe, Louis Hayward, Raymond Burr
Cinematographer: George Robinson
Columbia Pictures, 1948

SITE OF THE COMMUNIST SAFEHOUSE
153 Octavia Street, between Page and Rose Streets
Second floor, front apartment
Building since demolished

P ity the Communists of film noir. They always have to make things so difficult for themselves. In *Walk a Crooked Mile*, the very first red-scare film noir, a Soviet spy ring develops an intricate plan to smuggle nuclear secrets out of a high-security nuclear weapons plant in a small town outside of Los Angeles. They already have the key mole in place: a scientist who sits on the plant's central planning committee. Before the committee's weekly meeting, the mole dips his hand in a mysterious silver salt solution, and then presses his palm to the paper on which new nuclear equations are written. Then he presses his hand—wet with the solution—onto a white handkerchief, thereby imprinting the secret formula onto the handkerchief in invisible ink. The handkerchief goes through the plant's laundry system, is picked up by an unsuspecting secretary, sent to the dry cleaners, retrieved, and then picked up by another Communist agent—or something like that. Even upon repeated viewings it is rather difficult to follow the tortuous path taken by the secret formula, which, after all, is invisible. After these machinations the formula makes it into the hands of a Soviet spy in Los Angeles. But that's still not complicated enough: the spy then sends the formula, through a Soviet courier, up the coast to San Francisco. There the courier gives the formula to one Igor Braun, an urban landscape painter with French sensibilities. Braun writes the formula on a canvas, and then paints over it, so that the image can only be revealed when the painting is scanned with an infrared light. Braun then packs up the painting and sends it to

London. At this point we lose track of the formula for good, although we might assume that, after several hundred further transfers, it arrives at last in Moscow. Those filthy, tedious Commies!

Back in San Francisco, that Communist paradise, G-Man Daniel O'Hara (Dennis O'Keefe) and his partner Philip "Scotty" Grayson (Louis Hayward), a Scotland Yard investigator who is working with the F.B.I. through some kind of suspicious Anglo agent-exchange program, soon crack the Soviet plot. To do so they make use of some very clever technology; the Soviets's silver salt solution is nothing compared to the F.B.I.'s cutting-edge surveillance gadgetry. At a stakeout of Anton Radchek, a suspected Communist who is holed up in an apartment at 153 Octavia Street, agents connect the telephone wire to a recordable phonograph that presses records of every phone conversation, and they use a movie camera to film visitors to the building. (No trace of the Communist hideout exists today, though 157-159 Octavia Street bears a strong resemblance to the apartment in the film.) When the camera spots Radchek entering one night and not leaving for breakfast the next morning, O'Hara figures that something is wrong. Sure enough, Radchek is found dead in his room, reclining in his lazy chair. "Whoever killed him," concludes O'Hara, "he trusted." Unfortunately the F.B.I. had let the killer, a Communist spy dressed in a priest's habit, escape during the night. The pious G-Men could not conceive that a man dressed as a priest might be a fraud, let alone commit a crime. Pity the poor Americans, those gullible, God-fearing capitalists!

IMPACT:
THE BROCKLEBANK
APARTMENTS

Brian Donlevy, Mae Marsh, and Ella Raines in *Impact*, 1949. Photofest.

Director: Arthur Lubin
Cast: Brian Donlevy, Ella Raines, Helen Walker
Cinematographer: Ernest Laszlo
United Artists / Cardinal Pictures, 1949

THE BROCKLEBANK APARTMENTS
1000 Mason Street at Sacramento Street

How does one make a suspenseful movie that begins, and ends, with a close-up shot of a dictionary entry? Mal·a·droit·ly. The word in question is, of course, "impact," and its definition is spoken in a foreboding voiceover—twice. "Impact," says the stern lexicographer, is "the force with which two lives come together; sometimes for good, sometimes for evil." He alludes to the meeting of industry giant Walter Williams (Brian Donlevy) and pretty two-shoes Marsha Peters (Ella Raines), in the case of good; and Walter and his perfidious wife Irene Williams (Helen Walker), in the case of evil. Whatever dictionary the narrator might be consulting, it is not the new *American Heritage*, which defines the word as: "the striking of one body against another; collision." This definition is in fact even more appropriate for the film, since its most memorable scene does not involve an encounter between any of the three leads, but between a cream-colored Packard roadster and a high-octane gasoline tanker. In one of the most spectacular special effect sequences in all of 1940s film noir, the two vehicles smash head-on into each other on a winding mountain pass in the Sierra Nevada, explode in a huge fireball, and tumble headlong down a cliff. Now *that's* impact.

Irene and her lover have plotted Walter's death, and when the torched chassis of her husband's roadster is found, she assumes that her plot has gone successfully, if not exactly to plan. She assumes wrong. Following the recent examples of *Nora Prentiss* (1947) and *Bury Me Dead* (1947), *Impact* uses the bait-and-switch-the-charred-corpse gimmick, wherein the hero allows his enemies to believe that he has died in a fire that burned his body so severely that it cannot be identified. (Dental records conveniently do not exist in film noir.) Quincy, a wily Irish detective, fingers Irene for the murder, so Walter decides to hole up in a small town in Idaho while his deceitful wife takes the fall. There he meets Marsha Peters, a charmin' ole country lass whose stubborn honesty has a way of getting her in trouble—and Walter too.

Despite its hand-me-down noir plot *Impact* does make one contribution to the world of San Francisco noir. It is the first film to feature the Brocklebank Apartments, the striking L-shaped high-rise with a large brick-paved court that crowns the peak of Nob Hill. Built in 1924, the Brocklebank is a neighbor to the Fairmont and Mark Hopkins hotels, and is across the street from the old Flood mansion, which now houses the Pacific Union Club; all of these San Francisco landmarks can be seen in *Impact*, where they look very much the same as they do today. The Brocklebank would later appear in the television mini-series of Armistead Maupin's *Tales of the City* (1993), as Gene Wilder's apartment in the neo-noir satire *The Woman In Red* (1984), briefly in *Bullitt* (1968), where it is seen out of the window of Robert Duvall's taxicab, and most famously, in *Vertigo* (1958), as the home of Mr. and Mrs. Gavin Elster. In that film Scottie (James Stewart) sits in his car across Mason Street, waiting for Madeleine Elster (Kim Novak) to emerge from the courtyard's front pillars. Madeleine finally does, driving her green Jaguar past the Fairmont and taking a left down the hill at California Street. It is nearly a duplication of a stakeout scene in *Impact*, in which Quincy's police officers wait in the same spot across the street, watching for Irene in their rearview mirror. Irene walks out of the Brocklebank's courtyard and past the Fairmont, where she gets in a cab going down the hill at California. This is where the parallels end, however. In *Vertigo*, Scottie follows Madeleine to spectacular locations around the city, becoming increasingly mesmerized by her eerie behavior. In *Impact*, however, the cops trail Irene to a Western Union, where she is seen sending a telegram to her accomplice in the attempted murder of her husband. She's done for.

I MARRIED A COMMUNIST /
THE WOMAN ON PIER 13:
THE CENTRAL WATERFRONT

Richard Rober, Robert Ryan, and Laraine Day in
I Married a Communist / The Woman on Pier 13, 1949. Photofest.

Director: Robert Stevenson
Cast: Robert Ryan, Laraine Day, Thomas Gomez, Janis Carter
Cinematographer: Nicholas Musuraca
RKO, 1949

HARRY BRIDGES PLAZA
At the Ferry Building, on the Embarcadero at Market Street
THE PHANTOM PIER 13
On the Embarcadero, between Vallejo and Green Streets
THE STATION HOUSE OF THE BAR PILOTS
PIER 9
Closed to the public due to security concerns, but it can be viewed online
at the website of its architects, David Baker + Partners: www.dbarchitect.com

Although *The Woman on Pier 13* is the name that appears in the film's credits, this film may be better known by its original title, *I Married a Communist*. Both titles are misleading. Despite the fact that much of the film is set on the San Francisco waterfront, there is no specific mention of a Pier 13, nor does any woman step anywhere near any pier in the entire film. The woman to whom this title would seem to refer is Christine Howard (Janis Carter), a beautiful blond Communist agent who works as a journalist in the City. The second title is equally confusing, as it implies that the story unfolds from the perspective of another woman, Nan (Laraine Day), who unwittingly marries a reformed Communist, Frank Johnson (Robert Ryan). Johnson, not to be confused with the character of the same name in *Woman on the Run* (also 1950), is the film's traditional noir hero. He's a man with a checkered past trying to make good, who is sucked back into a seedy underworld of connivers and thugs. A better title for the film might have been "Better Dead than Red," a catchphrase that the film's screenwriters seem to have taken quite seriously, since every character linked to the Communist Party, no matter how tenuously, ends up dead. For Johnson, death does seem to be a relief from the torturous plight of Party life. He drifts off into the big sleep with a smile on his face.

Along with such titles as *I Was a Communist for the F.B.I.* and *The Red Menace*, *I Married a Communist* is one of a pack of red-scare noirs to emerge in the McCarthy era. It premiered just several months after

Joseph McCarthy publicly launched his anti-Red campaign with a speech in Wheeling, West Virginia, on February 9th, 1950, in which he accused more than 200 staff members of the State Department of being spies for the Communist Party. Although the film's propagandistic tone is chilling at times, it amusingly portrays the Communists not as Soviet apparatchiks or KGB spies but as your typical film noir gangsters. Thomas Gomez, who plays the character of Vanning, the leader of the Party's San Francisco cell, is a Raymond Burr knock-off; Janis Carter is a lanky, cut-rate Gloria Grahame. Vanning's henchmen strong-arm disloyal Party members into confessions and force them into "suicides." In one scene, Frank is shown what happens to those who cross the Party. Two Commie agents tie belts around an informer's arms and legs and punt him into the Bay, off of what we might assume to be Pier 13. The camera sadistically lingers over the flailing body as it plunges underwater, surfaces, and then sinks for good. These goons operate like any other mob, only they read Marx in their spare time.

The film's depiction of Communism does not so much take a critical view of Stalin's Russia as it evokes the fervor of American red-scare paranoia. The film's Communists never articulate their political theories or plans, and seem only interested in disrupting the labor negotiations between the stevedores and the big shipping companies on the San Francisco docks. Ironically, besides noir gangsters, the other characters the Communists in the film most resemble are the McCarthyites themselves. Vanning secretly follows his own Party members around the city, waiting for one of them to slip up or to betray him. At one point, his men yank Johnson out of a dinner party he is hosting and bring him to Party headquarters at the dock. When Johnson gets there he sees that he's at the back of a line of Party members being interrogated by Vanning. Vanning's men trust no one, especially those in their Party. They're haunted by the thought of American spies in their midst.

Vanning is an ugly caricature of the revolutionary San Francisco labor leader Harry Bridges, who organized the International Longshore and Warehouse Union in 1937 and served as its president for forty years. During his tenure he fought off several efforts, led by Attorney General Robert H. Jackson and endorsed by the San Francisco newspapers, to imprison and deport him for alleged ties to the Communist Party. He denied having cooperated with the Communists, however, and in two major cases the Supreme Court ruled in his favor. Still, the F.B.I. kept a case file on Bridges between 1940 and 1956 that ran to thirty-eight thousand pages. Finally, in 1958, Bridges was issued an American passport. After his death in 1990, at the age of 88, the area in front of the Ferry Building was officially named Harry Bridges Plaza.

Mysteriously, Pier 13 does not exist. In the space between Pier 9 and Pier 15 there is only a small parking lot and a canal filled with pilot boats from the Pier 9 station house of the San Francisco Bar Pilots. Founded in 1835, the Bar Pilots Association is the oldest continuously operating private enterprise in California. The bar pilots are responsible for guiding foreign vessels and any ships larger than 300 tons through the Bay. At all times a pilot is stationed twelve miles west of the Golden Gate Bridge, in the middle of the open sea, his boat tethered to a buoy on which "SF" is written in large letters. When a vessel, such as a container or bulk cargo ship, approaches the Bay, the pilot boards it by climbing up a rope ladder on the side of the ship. He takes control of the ship, which can be as large as a 1,000-foot supertanker, and guides it through the shallow horseshoe-shaped sandbar at the edge of the Golden Gate, negotiating high winds, strong currents, and thick fog. Some of the vessels follow narrow tributaries to ports as far east as Sacramento and Stockton, an operation that can take several days. These routes are some of the most dangerous shipping lanes in the country.

The pilots' station house, which won several awards for design excellence upon its completion in 1992, was built within the contours of a pre-existing 1932 industrial shed. Its steel trusses, concrete walls, and arched sash windows restored, the pilots' headquarters now resembles a luxurious fire station, with bunk rooms, a kitchen, a gym with steam rooms, game rooms, a library, offices, and a koi pond surrounded by giant bamboo trees.

THIEVES' HIGHWAY:
THE OLD PRODUCE DISTRICT

Lee J. Cobb and Richard Conte in *Thieves' Highway*, 1949. Photofest.

Director: Jules Dassin
Cast: Richard Conte, Lee J. Cobb, Valentina Cortese
Cinematographer: Norbert Brodine
20th Century Fox, 1949

MIKE FIGLIA'S MARKET
Corner of Washington and Davis Streets
FERRY PLAZA FARMERS MARKET
Ferry Building, the Embarcadero at Market Street
Tuesday, Thursday, and Sunday: 10 am–2 pm; Saturday: 8 am–2 pm
www.ferryplazafarmersmarket.com
☎ (415) 291-3276

After a grueling, all-day drive from Fresno, Nick Garcos (Richard Conte) rolls his truck into San Francisco's produce district in the middle of the night. Despite the late hour, a long line of fruit trucks stands bumper-to-bumper on Davis Street. Housewives comb the stands for deals on vegetables for dinner parties, while fruit-sellers and their henchmen (in the world of film noir, even the fruit-sellers have henchmen) gadfly about the trucks, looking to hustle the weary truckers for their fresh shipments of potatoes, strawberries, and peaches. But no one can compete with what Nick has to offer: two truckloads of luscious Golden Delicious apples, the first of the season. Unfortunately for Mike Figlia (Lee J. Cobb), the most prosperous and pernicious of all the fruit dealers, Nick isn't much interested in selling apples. He's after revenge. Figlia cheated Nick's trucker father, Yanko, out of a sale and then monkeyed with the brakes on his truck, a prank that cost Yanko his legs.

Figlia, however, sees Nick coming. When young Nick shows up at his store with all those fresh apples, Figlia hires a prostitute, Rica (Valentina Cortese), to distract Nick. Once Nick is up in Rica's room, Figlia sells Nick's apples behind his back, straight off his truck. Figlia's plan works— to a point. It's not just that Rica has a heart of gold, but that she takes a real liking to Nick, considers him a fellow traveler. (The film's Trotskyist undertones were inflammatory enough to get director Jules Dassin blacklisted in Hollywood. After *Thieves' Highway* he was forced to leave for London, where he went on to direct, most notably, *Night and the City* and *Rififi*.) Full of proletariat rage, Nick returns to the market and throws Figlia against the wall. He gets a better deal for the apples. Unfortunately, though, Nick's troubles have only just begun—Figlia and his henchmen don't take defeat from a hick apple-picker so easy.

Thieves' Highway provides the best visual record we have of the old San Francisco produce district, which was destroyed just ten years after the film's production. In 1959, the city's Golden Gateway Redevelopment Project demolished the "dilapidated, congested marketplace for wholesale produce" to make way for what is now known as the Embarcadero Center. Over the course of twenty-five years, the city built 1,400 new housing units (many in large apartment buildings), new park space and public plazas, and the three-and-a-half-million-square-foot Embarcadero Center shopping complex, which contains offices, restaurants, a hotel, and a multiplex movie theater. The only relic of the original produce market is an inconspicuous ivy-colored archway that now serves as the Front Street gate to the Sydney Walton Square Park, between Pacific and Jackson Streets.

The Embarcadero, however, remains one of the best places in the city to find fresh California produce. The Ferry Building holds an excellent farmers market four times a week, where regional farmers sell their own bounty, eliminating the middlemen—both the truckers and the grocers. Virtually everything for sale is organic and locally grown. Goat cheese comes from Petaluma, Armenian cucumber and heirloom radicchios from Corralitos, sweet cubanels and zapallitos from East Palo Alto, campanulas and sunflowers from Sebastopol, almonds and walnuts from Yolo County, and brick-oven sourdough bread from the Marin headlands. A farmer from Watsonville sells peppercress, red orach, amaranth, golden beet tops, dandelion leaves, and wild lambsquarters; a lavender farmer from Davis sells salt, sugar scrub, healing salve, honey, linen water, and sachets. A man from MacDoel, near Mt. Shasta, sells goat. But if it's apples you want, fresh Golden Delicious, make sure to visit at the beginning of fall. Talk to the man from Fresno.

TREASURE OF MONTE CRISTO:
THE HAAS-LILIENTHAL HOUSE

Glenn Langan and Adele Jergens in *Treasure of Monte Cristo*, 1949. Photofest.

Director: William A. Berke
Cast: Glenn Langan, Adele Jergens, Steve Brodie
Cinematographer: Benjamin H. Kline
Lippert Pictures, 1949

THE HAAS-LILIENTHAL HOUSE
2007 Franklin Street
The San Francisco Heritage Society leads
tours on weekends and on Wednesday afternoons
www.sfheritage.org / house.html#tours
☎ (415) 441-3000

Two happy-go-lucky sailors stroll through the Ferry Building just back from the war, beaming with hope and virility. "What'll it be?" asks the first sailor. "The girls or the gay time?" "Maybe a bit of both," jokes the second, the chipper Edmund Dantes (Glenn Langan).

An innocent response surely, with no innuendo intended, but as Dantes is soon to discover, San Francisco is no place for innocents. In his first hour on dry land he saves the beautiful Jean Turner (Adele Jergens) from two hoodlums (a term, incidentally, coined in Barbary Coast-era San Francisco). Over a drink with her he discovers that she has escaped from a mental asylum and is due to inherit her family's large fortune. She tells a convoluted story about being chased by killers eager to steal her inheritance. The bottom line is that she'll be killed unless she gets married in the next week. Anyone less gullible than Dantes wouldn't fall for it, but give him a break. He's been away from San Francisco for some time and has lost his savvy for detecting graft, even when it kisses him on the cheek.

The next morning they awake in a marriage suite at a Reno hotel. What's more, they've fallen for each other, fair and square. But their brief nuptial bliss is soon disrupted when Jean, utterly distraught for no apparent reason, asks Dantes to be a sweetheart and fetch her a pack of cigarettes. By the time he returns, there's no sight of the heiress except for a note, written in lipstick on the mirror. It gives the address of her mental asylum and the location of her room there: 2015 Franklin St.,

North Cupola. Then things get really insane.

At the corner of Franklin and Jackson, Dantes finds the building, an old Queen Anne Victorian. He climbs up the covered entrance to the second floor and crawls through the window. Jean isn't there, but there is a man—he seems to be a custodian of some kind—who begins to walk ominously towards Dantes. No sooner does the man ask an apprehensive, "Who's there?" than he gets lead poisoning courtesy of a second mystery man behind him, whose face we don't see. Dantes escapes but is apprehended by the police outside and accused of murder. He calls for his wife, Jean Turner, to save him, but when the heiress to the Turner fortune shows up at the police department, she is not his pouty blond newlywed but an older, sour-faced society woman who vehemently denies ever making Dantes' acquaintance. His Jean Turner does not seem to exist. And 2015 Franklin is not a mental asylum, but somebody's house. The gas chamber beckons.

2015 Franklin no longer exists, having been demolished in the 1960s to make way for a bland apartment building with obstructed views of the Bay. But next door, at 2007 Franklin, there still remains the Haas-Lilienthal House, which bears a remarkable likeness to its former neighbor, having been built in the same era (late nineteenth century) and in the same Queen Anne style. It is the only intact private home of that era open to the public. Like 2015, it has a large stairway leading up to the main entrance, shaded under a portico, as well as pointy wooden gables, a red brick chimney, and a single circular tower that, if the fog is dense enough, might be mistaken for a cupola.

CHINATOWN AT MIDNIGHT:
THE OLD CHINESE TELEPHONE EXCHANGE BUILDING

Hurd Hatfield in *Chinatown at Midnight*, 1949. Photofest.

Director: Seymour Friedman
Cast: Hurd Hatfield, Tom Powers, Jacqueline DeWit, Maylia, Ross Elliott
Cinematographer: Henry Freulich
Columbia Pictures, 1949

THE OLD CHINESE TELEPHONE EXCHANGE BUILDING
743 Washington Street, between Grant Avenue and Kearny Street
Built in 1909, by Kum Shu Loo
Now a branch office of United Commercial Bank

An interior decorator mentions in passing to her submissive boyfriend that she would like to have an expensive white jade vase. It seems they have some kind of arrangement worked out: she mentions an ornament repeatedly, he obtains it somehow, and she sleeps with him. The boyfriend, thin-lipped and catatonic, seems to be under the spell of a powerful sexual hypnosis. After hearing "white jade" for the fourth time, he heads over to G.L. Wing's Oriental Art store in Chinatown, where the vase is on display.

Unfortunately the premise of the tyrannical interior decorator and her sex-slave errand boy is not pursued, since things go very poorly at G.L. Wing's. Brandishing a pistol, the boyfriend, who is named Clifford Ward (though the name of the actor playing him, Hurd Hatfield, somehow seems more appropriate), holds up the store and ends up killing its two employees. When he delivers the vase to the interior decorator, she kisses him and promptly sends him on his way, much to his frustration.

After the initial murders, the action shifts to the police investigation, an extraordinarily tedious affair. The film unfolds like a standard police procedural, wherein every detail of the investigation is duly reported and exhaustively catalogued. We learn the dates and times of Clifford's every movement and follow the investigators as they pursue each tip-off and conduct each interview. After several setbacks, they visit a woman named Hazel Fong (Maylia), who works at the Chinese Telephone Exchange and received a call from G.L. Wing's on the night of the murder. Hazel's perfect memory of Clifford's voice ultimately leads to his capture.

Although it's hard to imagine that a switchboard operator at the Chinese Telephone Exchange—which is, as the film's voiceover tells us, the largest Chinese exchange "outside the Orient"—would remember a single man's voice, its operators were famous for their photographic memories. They spoke five Chinese dialects in addition to English, and knew the names and telephone numbers of the nearly 2,500 subscribers to the Chinatown telephone system. Callers would ring up the Exchange and simply ask for someone by name in order to be connected. To distinguish between multiple subscribers with the same name, the operators memorized their addresses and occupations. They also knew the names of every person who lived in each tenement, since buildings were often served by a single phone line.

In 1949, the year *Chinatown at Midnight* was released, the Pacific Telephone and Telegraph Company switched to the direct dial system and the exchange became obsolete. Although the building now holds a branch office of the United Commercial Bank, the building's exterior remains intact. The Exchange was designed to resemble a pagoda, with three bright green-shingled roofs curling upward at the edges, freshly painted red columns and stark vertical black plaques embossed with white Chinese symbols. The flamboyant pagoda is conspicuous on what is otherwise a faded street of old tenement buildings, electronics stores, and double-decker Chinese restaurants. On the wall behind the tellers inside the bank, the current owners have preserved a large design of two dragons snarling at a fiery sun.

D.O.A.:
THE CHAMBORD
APARTMENTS

Edmond O'Brien in *D.O.A.*, 1950. Photofest.

Director: Rudolph Maté
Cast: Edmond O'Brien, Pamela Britton, Luther Adler
Cinematographer: Ernest Laszlo
Cardinal Pictures, 1950

THE CHAMBORD APARTMENTS
1298 Sacramento Street at Jones Street
Building completed in 1922
James Francis Dunn, architect

"I don't think you fully understand, Bigelow," says the doctor to the panicked public notary who believes he has come down with a vile stomach flu. "You've been murdered." So begins Frank Bigelow's manic dash through San Francisco, as he searches for the man who has poisoned him. He soon realizes that someone has dropped the slow-acting "luminous toxin," a glow-in-the-dark poison, into his whisky at a bar on the Embarcadero. He has no more than a couple of days to live. Not exactly in running condition even before being slipped a Mickey, Bigelow (played with chubby élan by Edmond O'Brien) pinwheels his arms and bowls into dazed extras as he careens around the city in his desperate pursuit. Who, he wonders, would want to kill a poor public notary?

There's no simple answer. In fact, it's best not to try to sort out the byzantine plot turns that result in his murder, either here or while watching the film. Whereas many film noirs use plot twists and fast-paced chase scenes to keep the viewer's attention and advance the story, *D.O.A.* is held together primarily by moments, scattered throughout the film, of stupendous noir dialogue. The premise—that a murder victim stays alive long enough to avenge his own death—lends itself to a number of bizarre one-liners and inversions of normal noir conventions. In the film's famous opening scene, for instance, Bigelow stumbles into a police station to report a murder. Who was murdered, asks the police chief. "I was," Bigelow says. The police chief doesn't even raise an eyebrow.

The medical building in which Bigelow is diagnosed is not a medical building at all but one of Nob Hill's first apartment buildings, the Chambord Apartments. The ornate, sugar-white structure was designed by the obscure San Francisco architect James Francis Dunn, who died in October of 1921, six months before it was completed. Known as the "Wedding Cake building" for its wavy exterior, bowed-out balconies, and baroque ornamentation, the Chambord bears some resemblance to Antonio Gaudi's Casa Mila in Barcelona, which was built about ten years earlier. In the 1950s, just after *D.O.A.* was shot, the ornamentation was stripped from the building, supposedly because of seismic considerations. By the 1970s, the Chambord had deteriorated so much that neighborhood preservation groups had to fight to save it from demolition. In 1983, Fred Stimpson, a grandson of the building's earlier owners, commissioned a full restoration of the building, but the project stalled when its architects discovered that there existed almost no visual record of the original ornamentation. As a result, the fanciful ornamentation on the building today is modeled on only a few of Dunn's preparatory sketches and several grainy photographs. In fact, the brief glimpse of the Chambord Apartments in *D.O.A.* is one of the rare views of the building in its original condition.

WHERE DANGER LIVES:
THE LANNINGTONS'
SEA CLIFF MANSION

Faith Domergue, Robert Mitchum, and Claude Rains in *Where Danger Lives*, 1950. Photofest.

Director: John Farrow
Cast: Robert Mitchum, Faith Domergue, Maureen O'Sullivan, Claude Rains
Cinematographer: Nicholas Musuraca
RKO, 1950

THE LANNINGTONS' MANSION
112 Seacliff Avenue, between 26th and 27th Avenues

Robert Mitchum, who made a name for himself with his dazed, lethargic acting style, really out-Mitchums himself in *Where Danger Lives*. Here he's asked to play a man who, after getting walloped over the head by an iron fire poker, spends the rest of the film slowly slipping into a coma. The plot's suspense aside, we sit on the edge of our seats wondering how Mitchum, already slurred-voiced and heavy-lidded before his encounter with the fire poker, will manage to drift even further out of consciousness without dropping dead altogether. Mitchum's solutions are as gratifying as they are predictable: he garbles his speech even more, his head droops even lower, and he moves his limbs even less until, in the film's final scene, paralysis sets in.

Mitchum plays Dr. Jeff Cameron, a San Francisco doctor who provides generous care to his pediatric patients and even more generous care to his trusty nurse Julie Dawn (Maureen O'Sullivan, wife of director John Farrow and mother of Mia). Jeff's relationship with Julie is broken off, however, when he falls for Margo Lannington (Faith Domergue), a fast-times gal who lands in the hospital after an attempted suicide. But just as things seem to be going well with Margo, she abruptly dumps him, claiming that she must devote herself to caring for her over-protective father, Frederick Lannington (Claude Rains). When Jeff confronts the father at the Lanningtons' posh Sea Cliff mansion, however, he discovers that Frederick is not actually Margo's father, but her husband. A grisly three-way fight follows, in which Frederick rips an earring out of

Margo's ear, Frederick beats Jeff over the head with the aforementioned poker, and Jeff knocks out Frederick. Shortly afterward, much to Jeff's surprise, Frederick dies. The two lovers—one dazed by a concussion, the other, as it turns out, insane—head south for Mexico, reluctantly abandoning the posh Sea Cliff life forever.

Sea Cliff is a small, extravagant neighborhood tucked between Lincoln Park and the Presidio on San Francisco's north shore, just west of the Golden Gate Bridge. Each mansion peers just over the one in front of it, assuring each resident an unobstructed view of the Bay and the Golden Gate. 112 Seacliff Avenue does not exist, but there is a sizable gap—a driveway, a strip of grass, and a narrow cement path—between 98 and 120 Seacliff, on the north side of the curving road that runs along the Bay. That chink perfectly frames a view of the Golden Gate. If the Lanningtons did have a house in this plot, their view of the Bay would be as exquisite as any in the city. A view to kill, if not to die for.

WOMAN ON THE RUN:
LAUGHING SAL

Robert Keith and Ann Sheridan in *Woman on the Run*, 1950. Photofest

Director: Norman Foster
Cast: Ann Sheridan, Dennis O'Keefe, Ross Elliott, Robert Keith
Cinematographer: Hal Mohr
Fidelity Pictures Inc., 1950

LAUGHING SAL
at the Musée Mécanique
Pier 45 at the end of Taylor Street
Monday–Friday: 11 am–7 pm; Saturday–Sunday: 10 am–8 pm
☎ (415) 346-2000

L aughing Sal is an obese, larger-than-life-sized mechanical doll with red curls of real human hair, a slightly soiled smock, large freckles, and a ghastly gap-toothed smile. She stands hunched forward on top of a pedestal, her hands splayed out in front of her as if she's perpetually about to stumble forward, through the glass box that separates her from the weeping children and bemused adults who watch her, transfixed. For two quarters Sal, also known as the "Fat Lady," shudders to life and lurches forward and backward while a manic, disembodied laughter peals out from the glass box for minutes on end. In her new home at the Musée Mécanique, she seems meant to inspire awe and nostalgia, but the response she inspires most often in the museum's visitors is something more akin to dread.

No San Francisco landmark better suits *Woman on the Run*, a tender yet terrifying film noir that has been rediscovered by a new generation of film noir fans in recent years after having been forgotten for nearly half a century. The woman of the title is not so much on the run as is her husband, Frank Johnson (Ross Elliott); the story on which the film was based was named "Man on the Run," but Universal Studios' publicity department ordered the change because they wanted to showcase its star, Ann Sheridan, on the film's posters. After inadvertently witnessing a gangland slaying, Johnson is sought by the police, by the gangster against whom he will be asked to testify, by a persistent reporter, and by his wife, who must get him the medication he takes for a serious heart condition that is aggravated by stress. As tense as the premise is, the most memorable aspect of the film is its delicate portrayal of the relationship between the husband and wife, one of the more nuanced relationships in all of film noir. When the cops inform Eleanor Johnson (Sheridan) of her husband's disappearance, she reacts with such mild despair that it might easily be mistaken for indifference. When she is asked to supply a photograph of her husband, she replies that she has none. Yet as the film progresses, and she reflects on their life together, she remembers their former happiness and gradually falls back in love with him. The graceful depiction of their revived love affair is a remarkable feat, especially since the husband and wife don't appear in any scene together until the final minutes of the film.

Those final, harrowing minutes are set in Whitney's Playland amusement park at night, and are syncopated by a dive-bombing rollercoaster that thunders over the soundtrack at irregular intervals. Although most of *Woman on the Run* was shot on location in San Francisco, this final scene was actually shot at Ocean Park pier in Los Angeles—not that many contemporary viewers would be able to tell, since Playland was razed in 1972 to make way for beachfront condominiums. Only the final shot of the film, a close-up of Laughing Sal, was actually shot at Playland. And although it has nothing to do with the plot and appears only once in passing earlier in the scene, Sal's laughing face is the perfect expression of the film's haunting combination of glee and terror.

Laughing Sal and several of her mechanical colleagues, including the soothsaying Grandma, Drunk Dan, and Jolly Jack, are all that's left of Playland now. Having been restored to their original condition, they are on display at the Musée Mécanique, a free museum at Fisherman's Wharf that boasts of having "one of the largest privately owned collections of Antique coin-operated automatic mechanical musical instruments in the world." It is no minor distinction. For a quarter you can "See Susie Dance the Can-Can," or watch, through a viewfinder, a slide show of the 1906 Earthquake and Fire. Another viewfinder bears the elliptic title, "Don't Fail to See the 'Unknown'?" The slides that mechanically flap by every few seconds show a chorus girl in her changing room, striking suggestive poses despite being clothed from ankle to wrist. The slide show reaches its culmination with a topless nightclub act, photographed from the last row so that you can just make out a stage and one or two lascivious pixels of bare flesh.

As a token gesture to the current generation of coin-operated arcade games, the Musée Mécanique has crammed the back of its one-room museum with a sizable collection of contemporary video games. These games are almost completely ignored, not just by the adults but also by the many children who flock to World Series Baseball, a 1927 pinball game set at a miniature Yankee Stadium, and K.O. Boxers, in which two iron boxers punch each other until one is knocked down. And as loud as the new arcade games are, they are no match for Laughing Sal, whose ribald shrieks overwhelm her rivals' blips and zooms, intermittently filling the frenzied room with a sound that would be grotesque if it weren't so mournful.

THE MAN WHO CHEATED HIMSELF:

FORT POINT

Lee J. Cobb and Jane Wyatt in *The Man Who Cheated Himself*, 1950. Photofest.

Director: Felix E. Feist
Cast: Lee J. Cobb, Jane Wyatt, John Dall
Cinematographer: Russell Harlan
20th Century Fox, 1950

FORT POINT

Take Highway 101 North toward the Golden Gate Bridge, stay in the farthest right lane and take the "Last San Francisco Exit," just like Lee J. Cobb. Proceed through the parking lot to your right until you reach the stop sign (Lincoln Boulevard). Turn left and proceed to Long Avenue until it ends at the fort. Free and open to the public from Friday–Sunday, from 10 am–5 pm (limited hours due to the current retrofitting of the Golden Gate Bridge, which is scheduled to be completed in 2007)

In *The Man Who Cheated Himself*, Jane Wyatt, who would later attain national celebrity as Margaret Anderson, the prudent mother of *Father Knows Best*, plays Lois Frazer, a grossly imprudent femme fatale. Lois' marriage is not nearly as successful as Margaret's. She is blatantly unfaithful to her husband and wants to divorce him, but fears that he might kill her if she tries. So she panics and shoots him first. "I didn't know what I was doing," she says helplessly, begging her lover, homicide detective Lieutenant Ed Cullan (Lee J. Cobb), to save her. "Take a sedative," he says, while he disposes of her husband's corpse.

Wyatt is a terrible femme fatale. She promptly disregards whatever tasks Ed gives her—like hiding the bullet slug from her discharged pistol—with disastrous consequences. Nor is she particularly seductive; her sex appeal is more Barbara Billingsley than Gloria Grahame. Why, then, does the moody, appealing Lieutenant Ed Cullan risk his life for her? His brother, detective Andy Cullan (John Dall), asks him this very question. "Under the skin," replies Ed, with a resigned shrug. She gets under the audience's skin too. Like a wood tick.

Despite Lois' bumbling manner, Cobb's endearing, put-upon sulk and gorgeous location shooting by cinematographer Russell Harlan help to give *The Man Who Cheated Himself* an unexpectedly captivating, and tragic, conclusion. To escape from a police dragnet led by Ed's brother Andy, the two lovers head to Fort Point, an abandoned military base. It's late in the afternoon and the joints of the Golden Gate Bridge cast

73

jagged, crisscrossing shadows across the empty courtyard. Peering through a rifle slit from a room in the old officers' quarters, Ed spots his brother's police car approaching. As he rushes with Lois up to the fort's lighthouse her clattering heels, echoing like gunshots, give them away. (This was not a sound effect: due to a flaw in the fort's design, echoes had always been a problem. During its years of operation the noise of the firing cannons reverberated loudly off the red brick walls, causing numerous soldiers to go deaf.) Andy soon arrives, racing through the dark casements and the narrow passageways in the bastions, before spotting the lighthouse. Yet just as he nears the top, he realizes that he has trapped his brother. With a pained look on his face, he slowly retreats. Meanwhile Lois, irritated with all the bother and physical exertion, loudly complains that she's chilly. And then she drops her scarf. Ed watches with horror as it floats down to the courtyard, landing on the ground right next to Andy.

Fort Point rarely saw such excitement in its own time. Built between 1853 and 1861, just after California became the 31st state, it stood guard during the Civil War against ships invading from the South. But no enemy ship ever came. One Confederate raider, the CSS *Shenandoah*, planned to attack San Francisco in the summer of 1865, but cancelled its mission on the way to the harbor when the captain learned that the war had ended. Shortly thereafter, the fort fell into disuse. By the turn of the century, all 102 of its smooth-bore cannons had been dismounted and sold for scrap. In the following decades, the fort was used only intermittently, for storage and as a training facility. The lighthouse, however, was kept in operation. Aside from the 1906 earthquake, which caused only moderate damage to the fort, this most peaceful of military bases continued to see very little action, proudly earning its title as "A Fort That Never Fired a Shot in Anger." John Rankin, who served as the lighthouse keeper from 1878 to 1919, described fort life in a letter written at the end of his career:

> *There is nothing here to see. There is the ocean and the sand and the guns and the soldiers. That is all. It grows monotonous. Always the ocean and the sand and the guns and the soldiers. As for the ships, one grows tired of them, too. I have my family and my pleasures.*

Fort Point emerged briefly from retirement at the beginning of World War II, when an anti-submarine net was stretched across the Bay, from the fort to Lime Point on the Marin Peninsula. (No enemy submarine ever came.) After the war the fort was abandoned for good, and stood empty until 1970, when it was designated a National Historic Site. Today the Parks Service offers guided tours and exhibits on the lives of Civil War soldiers, which include photographs of them playing cards on the rooftop deck and spending long silent hours peering out at the empty Pacific. Several times a day, park rangers conduct cannon demonstrations. In these thirty-minute drills, cannons are cleaned, loaded, and—in the spirit of historical accuracy—unloaded.

THE HOUSE ON TELEGRAPH HILL:
JULIUS' CASTLE

Valentina Cortese and Richard Basehart in *The House on Telegraph Hill*, 1951. Photofest.

Director: Robert Wise
Cast: Valentina Cortese, Richard Basehart, William Lundigan, Fay Baker
Cinematographer: Lucien Ballard
20th Century Fox, 1951

Julius' Castle
1541 Montgomery Street at Greenwich Street
☎ (415) 392-2222

I n *The House on Telegraph Hill*, nothing is what it seems—even the orange juice. Take, for instance, this climactic confrontation between concentration camp survivor Karin (Valentina Cortese) and her creepy husband Alan (Richard Basehart), who she believes is trying to kill her:

ALAN: Don't forget your juice dear, it'll help you sleep.
KARIN: No, I don't think I want it tonight, it doesn't taste right.
ALAN: Why, what'sa matter with it?
KARIN: It seems…a little bitter.
ALAN: Bitter? [He pours himself a glass from the pitcher, sips.] Tastes fine to me. Come on dear, doctor's orders.
[Looking deep into each other's eyes, they gulp down their glasses of orange juice.]
ALAN: Come on dear, don't fight it, just close your eyes.

(*Several minutes later*)

ALAN [Mopping his brow and staggering down the stairs]: She's…poisoned me!

The orange juice is not the only thing suspicious in *The House on Telegraph Hill*. Alan is an impostor, posing as an enthusiastic father figure to little Chris, Karin's son and the heir to a great fortune; Margaret

(Fay Baker), the scornful governess, has a more intimate connection to the family than she lets on; Marc Bennett (William Lundigan), Alan's old friend, has motivations other than friendship for being close to Alan. But in many ways the basest fake of them all is our heroine, Karin. For she is not, in fact, Karin, but Victoria Kowelska, a close friend of the real Karin, who died in a Polish concentration camp during World War II. After stealing Karin's identification papers, Victoria adopts her friend's identity so that she can come to America instead of returning to her bombed-out Polish town. She lives opulently at the Telegraph Hill mansion belonging to Karin's family with Karin's young son, Chris, who has no memories of his real mother. To increase her chances of avoiding detection, Victoria decides to marry Alan, Chris's legal guardian. Alan is an unusual man. For one thing, he insists on drinking orange juice every night before he goes to bed. "Don't forget," he tells Victoria, by way of explanation, "I'm a native Californian."

Victoria is far more excited to see her magnificent house than she is to meet Chris, her "son." When she enters the mansion for the first time, she forgets all about the kid, who runs off upstairs. She stares mesmerized at the chandeliers, the fireplace, the rare vases and the cheval glass, the gilt-framed portraits of deceased family members, and the walnut davenport. Candelabras, giant bowls of flowers, and the grand stairway's chiseled pilasters cast ominous shadows against the paisley wallpaper. Bierznow is a distant, and inconvenient, memory.

The house on Telegraph Hill, as seen in the film, did not exist. The mansion was superimposed photographically on an actual site in Telegraph Hill, at 1541 Montgomery Street. As in the film, the property sits on a dead end above a cliff at the edge of Telegraph Hill. The actual building on the site is Julius' Castle, built in 1922 by the Italian immigrant and restaurateur Julius Roz. This pink building, adjacent to Coit Tower, is outfitted with red battlements, a stumpy tower posing as a turret, and panoramic views of the Bay. The dining room's décor matches that of the house in the film, with its dark wood wainscoting, green marbled columns, swirling brass metalwork, dowdy upholstered chairs, and long mirrors strategically placed to reflect the expansive view to those seated with their backs to the Bay. Since the restaurant is widely considered one of the most romantic dinner spots in the city, the maître d' advises making reservations for Valentine's Day dinner by mid-November. House specialties include the Colorado Rack of Lamb and the Crustacean Bouillabaisse, but impressionable viewers of *The House on Telegraph Hill* are advised to refrain from ordering the Blood Orange Sorbet.

THE RAGING TIDE:
PORT WALK NO. 14

Shelley Winters and Stephen McNally in *The Raging Tide*, 1951. Photofest.

Director: George Sherman
Cast: Richard Conte, Shelley Winters, Stephen McNally, Charles Bickford, Alex Nicol
Cinematographer: Russell Metty
Universal International Pictures, 1951

PORT WALK NO. 14
Follow the path from Jefferson Street behind Tarantino's

The Raging Tide is an excellent film noir for the first ten minutes, and a mawkish domestic melodrama (at sea) for most of the next eighty. Three-time loser Bruno Felkins (Richard Conte) guns down an associate in his Embarcadero office and sprints down to Fisherman's Wharf to hide from the cops, who have closed down the city (in a sequence that prefigures the opening minutes of *City on a Hunt*). At the Wharf he takes refuge on a fishing boat skippered by Linder (Charles Bickford), a lugubrious Danish fisherman who confuses his w's and v's, and his ingrate son Carl (Alex Nicol). The kindly Linder takes warmly to Bruno, who figures that the seafaring life might be just the thing for him. He comes to enjoy the decent, hardworking trade and the days spent outdoors, having spent his whole life as a crook in the San Francisco underworld. Apparently he's never even been out in broad daylight before. In one odd scene on the open sea, Bruno, stunned by the sight of the sun rising over the horizon, screams in terror.

Since Carl wants to try out the life of a gangster, Bruno trades him his extortion racket, a $200 weekly salary, and his wide-eyed girlfriend Connie (Shelley Winters) for a stint on deck his father's ship, the *Taage* (which means "fog" in Danish). The scheme works for a while, with Carl taking care of the dirty business while Bruno grows strong and tan in the salty Bay breeze. But running from the law in San Francisco isn't as easy as catching albacore. As Lieutenant Kelsey (Stephen McNally) says, "I'll never understand why a guy commits a crime in San Francisco. With only three exits, the guy should know he's a fly in a bottle."

Although much of the film's action takes place aboard the *Taage*, *The Raging Tide* is the film that, of the movies included in this collection, best captures 1950s Fisherman's Wharf. Director George Sherman lovingly portrays both the glitzy, touristy wharf that appears briefly in *Nora Prentiss* and the gritty docks featured in *The Midnight Story* and *The Woman on Pier 13*. Besides brief shots of the chock-a-block storefronts and crab stands that Bruno passes as he flees the cops, many scenes were filmed on the narrow wooden piers and on the small fishing boats in the harbor.

Many of these piers still exist, though they are now partially hidden by the seafood restaurants and tchotchke stores that line the waterfront. It's still possible to follow Bruno's escape route along the Wharf, and behind Tarantino's (on Jefferson Street at Taylor). There, an inconspicuous path leads to Port Walk No. 14, where dozens of small fishing boats still dock, tucked far behind the tourist-themed schmaltz of Fisherman's Wharf. Many of them are virtual replicas of the *Taage*, complete with rusty steering wheels, large clipper bows to deflect ocean spray, iron hawsers, chain fishing nets, and a small cabin just large enough to fit a father-son fishing team.

THE SNIPER:
THE PAPER DOLL CLUB

Marie Windsor and Arthur Franz in *The Sniper*, 1952. Photofest.

Director: Edward Dmytryk
Cast: Arthur Franz, Adolphe Menjou, Marie Windsor
Cinematographer: Burnett Guffey
Columbia Pictures, 1952

THE FORMER PAPER DOLL CLUB
524 Union Street near Grant Avenue

Everyone Eddie Miller (Arthur Franz) meets causes him misery: his pushy boss at the dry cleaning store; his unctuous, prying landlady; a mother who slaps her child on the street; a bickering teenage couple at the soda fountain; a bigoted socialite; a misogynistic male nurse who advises him on what qualities he should look for in a wife; and especially the lounge singer Jean Darr (Marie Windsor), who flirts with him just to get a discount on a dress she needs drycleaned. Eddie hates women, hates men, and, most of all, hates himself. His misanthropy is contagious, and spreads to the viewer. This is why Eddie himself, a serial killer who murders innocent strangers with a sniper rifle, emerges as the film's only sympathetic character. Just in case this wasn't clear already, director Edward Dmytryk ends the film with a stunning close-up on Eddie when he is finally caught by the dim-witted and sadistic police force. He is sitting on a bed in a cheap motel room, cradling his gun like a wounded child, a tear dripping down his nose.

There was good reason for Dmytryk to have taken such a spiteful view of American society. In 1947 he was one of ten members of the motion picture industry who refused to testify when called upon by the House Un-American Activities Committee (HUAC). Along with Ring Lardner Jr., Dalton Trumbo, and the seven other members of the "Hollywood Ten," he was convicted of contempt of Congress. He served a twelve-month sentence in Mill Point Prison, West Virginia. When he got out he found himself blacklisted in Hollywood, and moved to England (other blacklisted directors, like Jules Dassin and Cy Endfield, would soon follow). Low on cash and luck, however, Dmytryk sped back across the Atlantic and promptly scheduled a second discussion with the HUAC. He cleared his name by testifying against other members of the Hollywood Ten. *The Sniper* was the second film he made after his return.

The Sniper is an early example of the kind of film noir that became more common in the 1950s, and that looked ahead to later neo-noirs, like *Dirty Harry* (1971) and Peter Bogdanovich's *Targets* (1968), both portraits of a serial killer. *The Sniper* has no conventional bad guy, no murderous husband or organized crime ring. The shocking violence is not a means to an end, but the manifestation of larger societal impulses. In *The Sniper*, film noir's tense formula of paranoia, cruelty, and violence sprouts out of the underground and spreads through the city like a virus.

It's fitting that the city in which the film is set is never named. Even though it's clearly San Francisco, the script goes out of its way to avoid mentioning this fact. Take, for instance, the speech given by the police chief, when he refers to a previous spate of highly publicized killings several years earlier: "That was New York," he says, "this is here." The newspapers have no city names in their titles and the street addresses, which are sprinkled throughout the script, are false; Dmytryk films phony street signs with generic names like "Westwood Dr." and "Rector St." There is only one slip-up: the nightclub where Jean Darr sings. Although the name of the club is indecipherable when it appears in neon on the marquee, the small type on a police report reveals that it is the Paper Doll Club, which was located on the corner of Union and Grant. This is the site of the film's first, and most violent, murder. Having just left the club, Jean pauses in front of a poster advertising her appearance that night, looking at her own image behind the glass poster case and rubbing it for good luck. There is a loud blast as a sniper bullet sends her head crashing through the glass.

The Paper Doll was a real club in San Francisco in the 1940s and 1950s, and as in the film, musicians and singers, like Ann Weldon and Carmen McRae, performed there regularly. Although it's not clear in the film, the Paper Doll was also what the authors of *Where to Sin in San Francisco*, a 1948 guidebook, awkwardly called "a rendezvous of the Gay People." Today the old bar still stands, but it has no current tenant. It bears a striking likeness to the bar in the film, and can be seen through windows that look out on both Union Street and Cadell Place. Under the large blue awning, just to the left of the door, there are two small swinging doors cut into the wall. During times of operation, these doors opened to reveal a glass poster case advertising drink specials or that night's live performance or, for one night in 1952, the melancholy torch songs of a Miss Jean Darr.

SUDDEN FEAR:
IRENE NEVES' APARTMENT

Joan Crawford in *Sudden Fear*, 1952. Photofest.

Director: David Miller
Cast: Joan Crawford, Jack Palance, Gloria Grahame
Cinematographer: Charles Lang
RKO, 1952

THE TAMALPAIS APARTMENTS
1201 Greenwich Street at Hyde Street
Conrad A. Meussdorffer, architect
Built in 1923

It's unsettling to watch Joan Crawford sweat profusely, but perhaps that's the point. Dressed in a black fur coat and an oversized white scarf that's more burnoose than bonnet, she hides in the closet of her husband's mistress. In one white-gloved hand she clutches a revolver. She uses the other to stifle a scream while giant, glimmering beads of sweat collect across her forehead and nose. Will she pull the trigger? Will she lose her nerve? Will the plunk of falling drops of sweat give her away?

As frightening as Crawford may be in this moment, remarkably she is never as frightening as her two supporting actors, the reptilian Jack Palance and the fierce noir vixen Gloria Grahame. Crawford fought against casting Palance opposite her as the male lead, calling him the ugliest man in Hollywood. (Their on-screen relationship begins the same way: Crawford's character Myra Hudson, a celebrated playwright, refuses to let her producer cast Lester Blaine [Palance] as the male lead of her new play, saying that he's not "romantic enough.") Ultimately, however, *Sudden Fear*'s producer convinced Crawford that Myra had to be a sympathetic character, and that Palance was the only actor scarier than she was. Director David Miller puts Palance's surgically-reconstructed face—he suffered severe burns as a fighter pilot in World War II—to terrifying use. Neither Myra nor the audience can ever be sure what sinister motives lurk behind his taut, saurian features.

Still, in the world of film noir, it's usually because of a dame that the killing gets done. Lester would not have plotted to murder Myra were it not for the dark influence of his longtime girlfriend, Irene Neves (Grahame), who follows him from New York to San Francisco, hot for a big payoff. Grahame could play sultry, kittenish, or wicked but was best, as in *Sudden Fear*, when she played them all at once. Like the other characters in the film, we can never be sure of her intentions: does she imagine that inheriting Myra's fortune will enable her and Lester to elope together? Or, once they get the money, will she turn around and poison Lester, and make off with all the cash?

Irene's apartment at 1201 Greenwich, where Myra lays in wait for the plotting lovers, is the Tamalpais apartment building, the same building out of which Madge Rapf defenestrates in *Dark Passage*. Although it is unclear in *Sudden Fear*, the building is an eleven-story apartment house; Irene just happens to live on the first floor. It is in pristine condition today and within walking distance from Myra's mansion at 2800 Scott Street (formerly the home of legendary *Chronicle* columnist Herb Caen, and now the Indonesian Consulate) and just one block from Lester's apartment at the base of Lombard Street—the only street in the city crooked enough for the three of them.

CITY ON A HUNT/NO ESCAPE:
THE FLOOD BUILDING

Lew Ayres and Renny McEvoy in *City on a Hunt/No Escape*, 1953. Photofest.

Director: Charles Bennett
Cast: Lew Ayres, Marjorie Steele, Sonny Tufts
Cinematographer: Benjamin H. Kline
Lippert Pictures, 1953

THE JAMES C. FLOOD BUILDING
870 Market Street at the corner of Powell Street
Albert Pissis, architect
Built in 1904

City on a Hunt, an obscure but graceful noir directed by Hitchcock screenwriter Charles Bennett for the down-and-dirty Lippert Pictures, begins amiably enough. A friendly voiceover that sounds as if it belongs to a tour guide or real estate agent introduces the city over a montage of postcard images. "This is San Francisco," the voice says. "This is the Golden Gate Bridge. This is the Bay Bridge. Whether you live in a mansion on Nob Hill or in an old alley in Chinatown, you'll be happy just to be in San Francisco." We see the Ferry Building and behind it the gorgeous hills of Marin County and long to be transported back to the fancy-free life of San Francisco in the 1950s. A plum place to be…"UNLESS YOU COMMIT MURDER!"

The man's voice suddenly turns ugly and indignant as rather less charming images of the city flash by. He explains that when a killer is loose, the police clamp down on the city, closing the Golden Gate Bridge, the Bay Bridge, the Ferry Building, and the highways leading south. "Murderers," he gravely intones, "beware: San Francisco is the city of NO ESCAPE."

The washed-up songwriter John Tracy (Lew Ayres) is on the run, but he's an innocent man, a piano player guilty only of writing melancholy ballads and weeping into an empty bottle of bourbon. Fortunately for him, he's failed so thoroughly as a musician that the cops cannot even find any publicity photographs of him. They have only a broad physical description and his address. So Tracy decides to settle in the one place where he thinks he can't be found: among the crowds on Market Street. Only Pat Peterson (Marjorie Steele), who mistakenly believes that she's the killer—she socked the murder victim in the head earlier that night when he came on too heavy—knows what Tracy looks like and where to find him. She's got a guilty conscience and wants to help Tracy escape. She's also got a wandering libido, which helps Tracy in other ways.

Pat first spots Tracy at Simpson's Bookstore, at Market and Powell, but he soon bolts across the street to the Powell Street cable car turn-around, next to Woolworth's, which at that time had just opened in the Flood Building. Here, on the cable car, Pat finally catches up to Tracy and, much to his surprise, proposes that they flee to Mexico together. Just as they're speaking, however, a friend of her policeman husband recognizes her. She introduces Tracy as her cousin visiting from out of town. Her quick thinking saves Tracy for the moment but soon after, when her husband hears about the fictional cousin, the jig is up.

Now a city landmark, the Flood is a majestic, streamlined flatiron building that was the largest building in San Francisco upon its completion in 1904. Its columned, marble-floored lobby serves as the building's own miniature museum. Photographs on display there show the Flood Building at the time of its construction and two years later, after the great earthquake and fire. It was one of the few large buildings in the city to withstand the destruction, losing only several chips of the gray Colusa sandstone that covered its steel frame and brick curtain walls. (Owner James Flood was twice lucky, in fact: his enormous mansion at 1000 California Street also withstood the earthquake. Now home to the Pacific Union Club, it is one of the few original Nob Hill mansions still standing.) By just the next year, when much of San Francisco still lay in ruin, the Flood Building reopened, completely restored. In the eerie, apocalyptic photographs taken at the time, the Flood stands alone among the rubble of Market Street.

Dashiell Hammett was working in the Pinkerton Detective Agency's office in the Flood Building when he wrote *The Maltese Falcon*, and a replicate copy of the black, blunt-nosed falcon is on display in the lobby.

THE MIDNIGHT STORY:
CASA MALATESTA

Gilbert Roland and Tony Curtis in *The Midnight Story*, 1957. Photofest.

Director: Joseph Pevney
Cast: Tony Curtis, Marisa Pavan, Gilbert Roland
Cinematographer: Russell Metty
Universal International Pictures, 1957

CASA MALATESTA
1227 Montgomery Street at the Montgomery Overpass

A year before he starred in Billy Wilder's *Some Like it Hot*, Tony Curtis played another character who assumes a fake identity to trick criminal thugs. In *The Midnight Story*, the results are somewhat less cheery. After the murder of his childhood priest, Father Tomasino, traffic cop Joe Martini (Curtis) decides to infiltrate the family of the man he believes to be the killer, Sylvio Malatesta (Gilbert Roland). Sylvio takes pity on Joe, believing the boy to be homeless, and adopts him into his jovial Italian famiglia. Joe soon grows fat and comfortable, cozying up to Mamma Malatesta's cooking and cousin Anna's feminine figure in their beautiful house in North Beach.

Once Joe settles into the house, the action revolves around fairly mundane domestic melodramas: a dinner party in which the guests, a husband and wife, air their private quarrels; a big dance that Anna refuses to attend, despite her family's encouragement; and Joe and Anna's budding romance. Sylvio is at the center of it all, a warm-hearted, generous presence, betraying no sign of homicidal intent. And yet Joe's investigations into Sylvio's alibi and his relationship with Father Tomasino force us to question Sylvio's affability at every turn. As Joe keeps hatching new suspicions only to have them proven false, Sylvio's smiling volubility seems alternately sweet and menacing, switching back and forth so many times that we are made to question our own hunches. It's fitting that the family's name is a pun on *"mal di testa,"* Italian for "headache."

Like many of the late 1950s noirs, the film's mystery is internal and its trauma is psychological (as opposed to cranial). As Sylvio dispels each of Joe's doubts, we wonder which of the others might be guilty, and what further tragedy might be in store. Could the killer be Sylvio's tubby gambling friend, Charlie Cuneo? The demure Anna? Or maybe Joe himself? Everyone is a suspect—not because they all act suspicious, but because nobody does.

Most suspicious, however, is that house, which is clearly not in North Beach at all but perched on the edge of the Montgomery Street overlook. Although a fence has been erected around the property, it is still possible to see the old Victorian house through the slats, with its small garden and second-floor deck. During Joe's first night there he shares a cigarette with Sylvio on the overlook barricade, a view of downtown San Francisco behind them. The bottom half of Montgomery Street stretches out in a line of streetlamps that ends at the base of the Russ and Shell buildings. It would be difficult to fake a North Beach location there today, since one of the city's most recognizable landmarks, the Transamerica Pyramid, built in 1972, splits the view in half.

VERTIGO:
MISSION DOLORES

Kim Novak, *Vertigo*, 1958. Photofest.

Director: Alfred Hitchcock
Cast: James Stewart, Kim Novak, Barbara Bel Geddes
Cinematographer: Robert Burks
Paramount Pictures, 1958

MISSION DOLORES
Dolores Street at 16th Street
☎ (415) 621-8203

Alfred Hitchcock's San Francisco is almost unrecognizable from the San Francisco that figures so prominently in the many film noirs of the preceding two decades. Using VistaVision, an experimental 35mm color film format that yielded a wider aspect ratio and a sharper image, Hitchcock transforms the city from a dark, angular labyrinth to a bright fantasy of cloudy turquoises and blood reds. Gone are the steep streets, the blind alleys, the stilettos tripping down a hill in the middle of the night. In their place are the emerald Bay, the golden-lit Sequoia forest, and the lustrous white apartment buildings on Nob Hill. Even the night scenes—such as the opening rooftop chase at dusk or the brief shot of Union Square just before dawn—are not black but tinted with spectral blues and purples. After all, *Vertigo*, especially during the scenes in which Scotty Ferguson (James Stewart) trails the mysterious Madeleine Elster (Kim Novak) around the city, is as much a ghost story as it is a detective thriller. With *Vertigo* Hitchcock ruptured the limitations of classic film noir, proving that the crucial component of film noir was not its conventions of style or even plot, but its tone: that eerie feeling of dread spurred by a realization that the world is an unjust, sad, and violent place.

Hitchcock establishes this mood early on, when Scottie takes the assignment to follow Madeleine as she wanders around the city in a trance. She is obsessed (and perhaps possessed) by her great-grandmother Carlotta Valdes who, after losing her child, went mad and committed suicide a century earlier. Madeleine stares at a portrait of Carlotta at the Palace of the Legion of Honor in Lincoln Park and sits in the bedroom window of Carlotta's old Victorian mansion (the Portman Mansion at 1007 Gough, since demolished). She even attempts to kill herself, jumping into the Bay at Fort Point. Above her the Golden Gate Bridge gleams copper-red; shot from directly below, the bridge is as imposing and ominous as it has ever appeared on screen.

The most haunting moment in this sequence takes place, fittingly, at a graveyard. A ghostly haze suffuses the scene, blurring the sunlit monuments and gravestones. The cemetery's yellow tulips, carmine rose bushes, unevenly manicured hedges, crawling vines, and cypress trees obscure from Scotty (and the viewer) the sight of Madeleine visiting Carlotta's grave at the Mission Dolores Cemetery. From afar she seems immaterial, evanescent. We are made to wonder whether she is there at all.

The Mission Dolores Cemetery is one of two remaining cemeteries in San Francisco (the other is in the Presidio) and one of the few landmarks extant from the era in which Carlotta lived, the early nineteenth century. Spanish soldiers built the first church on the site in 1776, five days before the signing of the Declaration of Independence. The adobe Mission Dolores church that stands today was built in 1791. It is the oldest intact building in San Francisco and the oldest church building in California. In the years since the filming of *Vertigo* the graveyard has barely changed at all. Only Carlotta's headstone, constructed for the film, is no longer there—though it did stand on the grounds for twenty years after the film's production. Those actually buried in the cemetery include a French family killed in the explosion of the steamboat *Jenny Lind* in 1853 and Charles and Belle Cora, early San Francisco celebrities who ran the city's finest parlor house. The oldest marked grave belongs to Don Luis Antonio Argüello (1784–1830), the first governor of Alta California under Mexican rule. He is buried under the obelisk in the middle of the graveyard.

THE LINEUP:
THE SUTRO BATHS

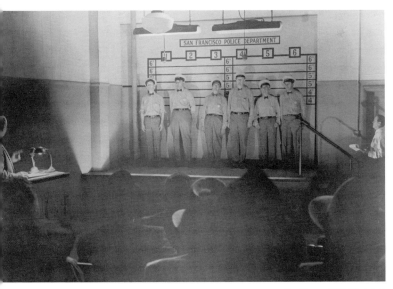

The Lineup, 1958. Photofest.

Director: Don Siegel
Cast: Eli Wallach, Robert Keith
Cinematographer: Hal Mohr
Columbia Pictures, 1958

THE RUINS OF THE SUTRO BATHS
At Point Lobos, in the cove next to the Cliff House
Follow the trails from the parking lot at El Camino
del Mar and Point Lobos Avenue

One expects to encounter urban ruins in cities like Rome, or Athens, or maybe even Detroit. But San Francisco? It's a city that abhors ruins, cleaning up after earthquakes and fires with the zeal of a diligent housekeeper, eager to prove its resolve in the face of disaster. This is the city, after all, that began running streetcars again just ten days after the 1906 earthquake, through streets lined with piles of rubble and blackened debris.

The Sutro Baths, however, are a conspicuous exception. In 1896, millionaire Adolph Sutro modeled his Baths after the Roman baths, but built his even bigger. Enclosed in a massive Crystal Palace-like glass and iron structure, the Baths contained seven swimming pools, making it the largest natatorium in the world. Lifeguards paddled in rowboats down the five-hundred-foot-length of the L-shaped pool, often supervising more than one thousand swimmers at a time. The Baths had 20,000 bathing suits and 40,000 towels available for rent, and five hundred heated and brightly-lit dressing rooms, equipped with showers. Alongside the main pool were six additional pools, heated to various temperatures and reserved for different uses. An intricate tunnel system pumped saltwater in from the ocean to all the pools (except for one that contained fresh water), recycling the water every hour. The grandstands surrounding the pools accommodated the crowds, as large as 7,000 people, who came to attend carnivals, festivals, and swimming championships. The structure housed three restaurants, a museum, and a Ferris wheel, and was crammed full of elaborate statuary, tropical plants, fountains, Egyptian mummies, trapezes and toboggan slides, diving boards and swinging rings, mechanical bucking broncos, paintings, totem poles, knights' armor, and displays with rare coins and valuable state papers. Stuffed animals lurked in hallways and in pavilions: an ox six feet high at the shoulder, an anaconda, a jaguar, owls, monkeys, and even exotic insects, delicately pinned up in glass cases.

When the Baths' novelty wore off in the 1950s they were transformed into a single gargantuan ice-skating rink, and enjoyed a brief prosperity in this new incarnation. It again became a popular destination for schoolchildren, romantic teens, and, as it appears in Don Siegel's *The Lineup*, a safe place to pass fat bags of uncut heroin, smuggled from the Orient, to evil crime bosses in wheelchairs.

Made in 1958, at the tail end of the classical noir era, *The Lineup* combines humdrum elements of earlier noir (the plodding police investigation, conducted by fastidious, by-the-book detectives) with the black humor of later films like *Point Blank* (1967) and Robert Culp's *Hickey and Boggs* (1972). While Siegel includes the bland, but ultimately effective detectives, he also gives us three of the most memorable, and inscrutable, crooks in all of film noir. Two of these are an older, effete man, Julian (Robert Keith), and his criminal prodigy, an irascible thug who calls himself Dancer (Eli Wallach). Julian has never committed an act of violence himself but meticulously plans the pair's murders with an implacable, calculating logic. Dancer is the triggerman, a hot-headed psychopath who makes up in bloodlust what he lacks in social grace. An anonymous organization sends them on a mission to recover bags of heroin smuggled from China in the luggage of unsuspecting American tourists on board a cruise ship. One after another, Julian and Dancer locate their marks, following them around San Francisco, repossessing the heroin and killing the witnesses. Their rampage takes them to the sauna room at the Seamen's Club, a mansion at 2090 Jackson Street, the Steinhart Aquarium, and finally the Mark Hopkins Hotel, where everything goes wrong. There they discover that the final bag of heroin is gone—a young girl had found it in her new Chinese doll and used its contents to powder the doll's face.

At Sutro's, Dancer must explain the missing bag of heroin to the big boss of the organization, a man about whom nothing is known except for his name: The Man. When Dancer finally meets him he is sitting on a balcony above the ice-skating rink in a wheelchair. As it turns out, The Man is elderly and crippled. He sits motionless as Dancer tries desperately to explain himself, using all the charm and refinement that Julian has taught him. When The Man finally speaks, he says just two words: "You're dead."

Just eight years later, in 1966, Sutro's would be hit by a real-life tragedy. The struggling business was about to file for bankruptcy when a mysterious fire burned down the whole structure. The owners collected a prodigious insurance settlement and fled the city. The ruins of the Baths were left alone and have stood there ever since, in the hollowed-out cove behind the Cliff House.

The stone remains of the Baths are filled with ocean water, though it is now brackish and murky, and the lanes separating the large L-shaped pool from the other, smaller pools are still visible. Remnants of the grandstands and fallen columns can be seen around the pool, overrun by odd white flowers and wild brush. At the north end of the cove, follow a damp tunnel through the cliff. Halfway through the passage there is a crevice in the rock wall through which you can see the surf rush into a secret inlet, bathed in a dark blue light even in the middle of the day. It is here where lovers, who once went on dates to the Sutro Baths, riding in the Ferris wheel and skating among the stuffed menagerie, now rendezvous at night, their voices inaudible under the sound of the breaking Pacific.

PORTRAIT IN BLACK:
THE JAPANESE
TEA GARDEN

Sandra Dee, Virginia Grey, and John Saxon in *Portrait in Black*, 1960. Photofest.

Director: Michael Gordon
Cast: Lana Turner, Anthony Quinn, Richard Basehart
Cinematographer: Russell Metty
Universal, 1960

THE JAPANESE TEA GARDEN IN GOLDEN GATE PARK
Located just east of Stow Lake, between JFK and
Martin Luther King Jr. Drives
Open daily, 8:30 am–5:30 pm

T he meandering garden paths lead to strategically secluded cul-de-sacs, the waterfall drowns out the sound of furtive whispering, and the murky green pond tells no secrets. The Japanese Tea Garden is, in short, a fine place to hold a secret rendezvous.

This fact is not lost on San Francisco widow Sheila Cabot (Lana Turner), who must meet in secret with Dr. David Rivera (Anthony Quinn), her lover and accomplice in the murder of her husband. After killing the elderly shipping magnate Matthew S. Cabot (Lloyd Nolan), the two guilt-ridden conspirators plan to live out the rest of their days traveling around Europe, supported by the Cabot fortune. Yet just when they think they've gotten away with it, Sheila receives an anonymous note at the Cabot mansion. Written in childish block letters, it says only:

Dear Mrs. Cabot,
Congratulations on the success of your murder.

David tells Sheila to meet him in the Japanese Tea Garden. Panic-stricken, they huddle under slanting red pines and dodge a nosy park guard as they try to figure out who wrote the anonymous letter. David insists that whoever the blackmailer is, he is bluffing. After all, nobody, besides the two of them, could possibly know about their crime or their adulterous affair. Sheila grimly agrees, but the horrified expression on her face reveals that there is something she is withholding. When David concludes that their tormentor must be close by, only Sheila knows exactly how close.

Portrait in Black was made just after the close of the classic noir era, a particularly awkward period in the noir canon. Noir needed to take a new direction, but it wasn't yet clear which direction, if any, this would be. The filmmakers and studios that still dared to make these films felt compelled to contemporize the classic formula in some way to make it appealing to viewers bored with standard noir conventions: they wanted noir with a twist. This strategy yielded mixed results. It emboldened several directors to create strange, innovative films that owed their pedigree to noir but veered off, usually with manic glee, into previously forbidden terrain. Sam Fuller, for instance, made *Shock Corridor* (1963) and *The Naked Kiss* (1965), films which take noir's fascination with psychosis and sexual degeneracy to new levels of depravity, following Alfred Hitchcock's example in *Psycho* (1960); John Frankenheimer focused on themes of paranoia and political disillusionment in *The Manchurian Candidate* (1962); and Blake Edwards turned to nostalgia and ultimately satire in *Experiment in Terror* (1962), with less success. *Portrait in Black* was a more misguided experiment, an ill-fated attempt to meld classic noir with another expiring genre, the lush Technicolor melodrama (Douglas Sirk's final feature film, *Imitation of Life*, also starring Lana Turner, was released a year earlier, in 1959). *Portrait in Black*'s failure was productive at least, effectively killing both genres at once.

EXPERIMENT IN TERROR:
CANDLESTICK PARK

Glenn Ford in *Experiment in Terror*, 1962. Photofest.

Director: Blake Edwards
Cast: Glenn Ford, Lee Remick, Ross Martin
Cinematographer: Philip H. Lathrop
Columbia Pictures, 1962

CANDLESTICK PARK
Home of the San Francisco Giants, 1960–1999, and current
home of the San Francisco 49ers
Take the Candlestick Park Exit off of Highway 101 South, to
Giants Drive at Gilman Avenue

xperiment in Terror is Blake Edwards' only experiment in film noir, a genre that by 1962 had become somewhat passé, associated with a post-war period that was rapidly receding into the past. Despite several moments of high tension, the quality most prevalent in Edwards' film is not terror but a somewhat confused nostalgia for early film noir. In the spirit of homage, he films in black and white and casts the stern-eyebrowed Glenn Ford, who had not made a noir since *Human Desire* (1954), as a virtuous F.B.I. agent. And while Edwards does incorporate real elements of noir—high camera angles, an expressionistic use of shadows, the constant threat of brutality—the film shuttles between nostalgia and its inverse: farce. (Edwards would go on to specialize in farce for much of his career, most notably with *The Pink Panther*, *The Great Race*, and *What Did You Do in the War, Daddy?*) In *Experiment in Terror*, nothing is as grim as the film's plot would make it seem.

"Red" Lynch (Ross Martin), a heavy-breathing rapist and killer, forces doe-eyed bank teller Kelly Sherwood (Lee Remick) to steal $100,000 from the Crocker-Anglo National Bank (now the Wells Fargo at Montgomery and Post Streets)—or else he'll kill her and her sixteen-year-old sister, Toby. Yet Edwards makes sure we don't take this frightening scenario too much to heart. Lynch's gruesome, wheezing breath, which we hear long before we even see his face, is not so much sinister as it is clinical: the man is an asthmatic, a fact we realize when Edwards shows him huffing from a pocket inhaler. Later, after a particularly suspenseful scene, we're shown a close-up of young Toby screaming bloody murder—but then the camera zooms back, and we see that she's only jumping from a high dive at the neighborhood swimming pool. Bodies hanging upside down from a ceiling turn out to be mannequins (a restaging of the scene at the mannequin factory in Stanley Kubrick's *Killer's Kiss* [1955]), and a fist flying straight into the camera introduces a brief scene set, for no apparent reason, in a karate class. Edwards knows that his audience, having just sat through two decades of film noir, expects the worst, and he toys with these expectations. If we're jolted by his visual prestidigitation, the joke's on us.

Nowhere does Edwards use such a calculated, jocular approach as in the film's climactic scene at Candlestick Park. Lynch arranges to pick up the $100,000 from Kelly at a sold-out baseball game, while John Ripley (Ford) and dozens of other F.B.I. agents patrol the stadium for the killer. Edwards repeatedly draws our attention away from the cat-and-mouse game between the killer and the F.B.I. agents, however, and toward the other game that is unfolding—the ballgame between the Giants and their California rivals, the Los Angeles Dodgers. By the time we're in the late innings, Kelly seems to be the only one in the ballpark (including Edwards) who is more anxious about her impending encounter with the asthmatic killer than about the struggles of the Giants' pitching staff. While she nervously scans the stadium for Lynch, the fans around her ignore her completely, cheering and booing and eating hot dogs. Even the F.B.I. agents seem distracted from their vigil by a disputed call at second base. The camera doesn't pay much attention to Kelly either, as Edwards lingers longingly in close-up on Don Drysdale, who stares down from the mound at Giants hitters Felipe Alou, Willie McCovey, and Willie Mays. The soundtrack is not a suspenseful orchestral suite but Vin Scully's play-by-play call (a somewhat odd choice if only because Scully is the Dodgers', not the Giants', broadcaster). Although the lives of Toby and perhaps Kelly hang in the balance, Edwards' message is clear and reassuring: the scene, and the film itself, is a kind of game that, as Ripley confidently assures Kelly, will be won by the good guys. This marks a major departure from the earlier, classic noirs, which were pervaded by a sense of impending doom. Here fate ticks calmly toward an inevitably happy resolution. As a result the action is fun and exciting, like a good baseball game—but not terrifying.

That isn't to say that baseball games at Candlestick were never themselves experiments in terror. When the Giants moved to San Francisco in 1958, the city decided to build its new stadium on Candlestick Point, one of the foggiest and chilliest spots in America on a summer night. Thirty-mile-per-hour gales blew in from left-centerfield and out toward right at all times, blasting those seated in the upper levels and costing Willie Mays, by his own count, 200 home runs over the course of his career. Although Richard Nixon, who threw out the first ball at the 'Stick on April 12, 1960, called it "the finest ballpark in America," San Franciscans were usually less sanguine: Herb Caen called it "the ninth blunder of the world" and Giants' vice-president Pat Gallagher likened playing at Candlestick to "playing on the deck of the aircraft carrier *Enterprise* in the South China Sea." In the 1961 All-Star Game, Giants pitcher Stu Miller was called for a balk when the wind knocked him out of his set position, and in 1963, during the visiting New York Mets' pre-game batting practice, a particularly strong gust lifted up the batting cage and deposited it sixty feet away, on the pitching rubber. The most frightening moment, however, occurred on October 17, 1989, while a sold-out crowd of 62,000 people awaited the beginning of the third game of the World Series between the Giants and the Oakland Athletics. The Loma Prieta earthquake shook the stadium for fifteen seconds, causing the concrete slabs above the upper deck to separate by several feet and slam back together, the lighting poles to sway wildly back and forth, the top deck above centerfield to teeter precariously, and the field, in the words of one fan, to roll "as if it were an ocean, moving like a wave, just like water; waves and waves and waves." But Candlestick held, the crowd cheered, and the World Series resumed ten days later.

POINT BLANK:
ALCATRAZ

Sharon Acker, John Vernon, and Lee Marvin in *Point Blank*, 1967. Photofest.

Director: John Boorman
Cast: Lee Marvin, Angie Dickinson, John Vernon, Carroll O'Connor
Cinematographer: Philip H. Lathrop
MGM, 1967

ALCATRAZ TOURS
Including the night tour and the circumnavigational boat tour
Ferries depart from pier 41, at Powell Street and Fisherman's Wharf
Blue & Gold Fleet
www.blueandgoldfleet.com
☎ (415) 705-8200

O f all the films that have been shot, or set, at Alcatraz, none better captures the Rock's overwhelming sense of dread and isolation than *Point Blank*. Yet unlike films such as *The Birdman of Alcatraz, Escape From Alcatraz, Murder in the First*, and *The Rock, Point Blank* barely takes place on the island: only the opening scene is shot there. *Point Blank* is not even set in the period (1934–1963) during which Alcatraz was a federal prison. By the time the film was made in 1967, Alcatraz was an abandoned ruin. But in the film's final shot, when director John Boorman pans up from Fort Point, over San Francisco's skyline and into the Bay, resting finally on Alcatraz, the island takes on an aura of mute, all-consuming dread that no cinematic depiction of its prison life, no matter how cruel, has ever achieved.

In the film's first scene, Walker (Lee Marvin), his wife Lynne (Sharon Acker), and his friend Mal Reese (John Vernon) ambush several drug dealers who are using the abandoned island as a secret drop-off point. When Mal discovers that they've made less cash than he had expected, he decides to cut Walker out of the operation. After shooting him repeatedly—at point blank range—in one of Alcatraz's 6'x6' cells, Mal runs off with Walker's wife and all the cash: $93,000, a figure invoked so frequently throughout the film that it assumes the gravity of a religious mantra. A year later Walker resurfaces in San Francisco, on the circumnavigational boat tour of Alcatraz. Surprisingly he doesn't much care about seeking revenge on Mal, or even about finding his traitorous wife.

Walker simply wants what's rightfully his: the $93,000. Ghostly and implacable, he follows his mission to its bloody conclusion.

Or does he? Boorman's hallucinatory style and the ambiguities of the plot leave the viewer with a number of possible interpretations of the film. Are we really to believe that Walker, ballasted with lead (and relieved of a massive quantity of blood), actually made the treacherous swim across the Bay, a swim which (as the tour boat's guide reminds us) no Alcatraz escapee ever survived? Perhaps we're to take Chris (Angie Dickinson) literally when she tells Walker, "You died at Alcatraz all right." It is worth noting that, despite the manifold violence wreaked by Walker and the explosive torrents of bullets fired from his .38 (at the time, the biggest revolver ever to have appeared on the big screen), he does not actually shoot anyone himself. For that matter, he does not even commit a single murder, at least not directly. Walker's victims commit suicide, stumble off of balconies, and shoot each other. These clues suggest that Mal, and the mysterious Organization that employs him, have not so much been avenged by Walker as haunted by his ghost.

Yet the final, lingering shot of the prison suggests a third interpretation: Walker has not come back at all, in any form, and the film is simply the nightmarish ravings of a dying man. It's an interpretation borne out by Boorman's hallucinatory, fragmented style, in which reason gives way to an impeccable dream logic based on association and memory. Walker moves through his dream like an automaton, his emotions not expressed in his behavior but manifested visually, in bright, over-ripe colors. He does not react to Lynne's suicide, but simply stares at her broken perfume bottles in the sink, swirling oily green and red. In a violent fight at a nightclub called the Movie House, Walker's face is stolid, but turns alternately pale and flushed under the club's flashing lights. The cell-block's bars enter the delirious man's fantasy in the form of the shadows of freeway columns, blinds, and construction scaffolding that constantly drift across his face.

The film's conclusion leaves us with the unsettling realization that, despite the film's hysterical pace and the far-flung path taken by Walker's vengeance, we have never actually left Alcatraz. Like Machine Gun Kelly, Alvin "Creepy" Karpis, and Al Capone, Walker is stranded on the brutal island, consumed by his vivid imagination and his regret.

BULLITT:
THE CHASE

Steve McQueen's Mustang fastback in *Bullitt*, 1968. Photofest.

Director: Peter Yates
Cast: Steve McQueen, Robert Vaughn, Jacqueline Bisset
Cinematographer: William A. Fraker
Solar Productions, 1968

THE CHASE
Bernal Heights, North Beach, Potrero Hill, Nob Hill,
the Embarcadero, the Marina, Highway 1

The elements of a great car chase scene are by now well established. They include, in descending order of importance: explosions, loud sound effects (usually explosions but also brakes and secondary collisions), screeching 180s (often resulting with objects in close proximity exploding, such as plates of glass or large stacks of paint cans), cars crashing into each other and exploding, flying cars, off-road driving, near-collisions, swerving around obstacles, duration, and beautiful scenery. The chase scene in *Bullitt*, which is among the most famous car chase scenes in film history as well as one of the best, has only a few of these elements, and those it does have are represented minimally. There is only one explosion, for instance, and it comes at the very end of the scene. No pedestrian cars get damaged significantly; a biker does fall off his motorcycle, but we see him dust himself off and walk away safely. Until the final explosion, the cars keep to the asphalt, except for a brief spin-off onto the highway shoulder by Lieutenant Frank Bullitt's (Steve McQueen) forest green Mustang fastback. But he only does this out of charity: he wants to avoid running over the motorcyclist. The cars don't jump as high off the roads as might be expected, given the many steep hills they bounce over. At one point it even seems that the lead car, a Dodge Charger, *slows down* over a steep hill so as not to bruise its undercarriage.

Yet the chase remains a visceral and technical masterpiece, and certainly the best scene in the film. In large part this is because it's the only scene where McQueen shows any hint of emotion (through the rest of the film he wears a single expression of tense weariness that cannot be shaken by abuse, violence, or even a half-naked Jacqueline Bisset). This is not to say that he acts any differently in this scene—his face is no more animated than a stunt driver's—but the machine, the fastback, assumes all the fury that his blank demeanor wants. Viewers sometimes forget that when the scene begins on Army Boulevard (now Cesar Chavez), the Organization's henchmen are chasing Bullitt. He leads them up Bernal Heights, disappears, then magically reappears in the Charger's rearview window—the pursued now the pursuer. With this nifty reversal the fastback reclaims the city from the Organization, who are, after all, outsiders (earlier in the film Bullitt learns, with some disgust, that they're from Chicago). As the fastback careens around corners and bounces over hillcrests, it literally drives the Organization's men out of the city, slowly but methodically. They head east to Potrero Hill, skirt the Bay on the Embarcadero, then drive south on the Guadalupe Canyon Parkway in Daly City before they slide off the road and collide into a gas station, yielding that single cathartic explosion. We see burning carcasses entombed in the jagged frame of the Charger, but not Bullitt's reaction. In the next shot we're back in the city, the fastback cruising home, bobbing triumphantly over a little hill on its way back to the police station. It's the closest that Bullitt ever comes to a swagger.

DIRTY HARRY:
KEZAR STADIUM

Clint Eastwood in *Dirty Harry*, 1971. Photofest.

Director: Don Siegel
Cast: Clint Eastwood, Harry Guardino, John Vernon, Andy Robinson
Cinematographer: Bruce Surtees
Warner Bros./The Malpaso Company, 1971

KEZAR STADIUM
At the corner of Frederick and Stanyan Streets

In early film noir, shadowy hit men and devious masterminds tend to lurk in alleys, side streets, and underground warrens. They lure the hero into the depths of their underworld where, hidden from the public eye and the nearest cop's beat, they can attack with impunity. Think of Miles Archer getting clipped in Burritt Alley in *The Maltese Falcon*, the dead end cul-de-sac where Frank Johnson witnesses a gangster's murder in the first scene of *Woman on the Run*, or the Hall of Mirrors scene in *The Lady from Shanghai*, in which a tiny, enclosed space converges on itself ad infinitum.

Dirty Harry is about a new kind of killer, one who has clawed his way out of the underworld and terrorizes wide-open public spaces. By 1971, the year the film was made, serial killers had captured the popular imagination with a series of highly publicized and grisly murders. The Boston Strangler murdered thirteen women between 1962 and 1964; Charles Whitman shot forty-four people from the top of the bell tower at the University of Texas in Austin in 1966; Charles Manson and his Family prowled Hollywood in 1969; the Son of Sam terrorized New York in the summer of 1970; and the Zodiac killer, on whom the character of serial killer Scorpio in *Dirty Harry* is based, committed a string of seemingly random murders in San Francisco from 1968 to 1970. Serial killers had been the subjects of film noirs as early as *The Sniper* (1952), but Scorpio (Andy Robinson) has little in common with *The Sniper*'s Eddie Miller (Arthur Franz). Eddie chooses his victims deliberately and kills on empty streets, usually at night. Scorpio, on the other hand, seems to delight in the very randomness of his murders. Like the Zodiac Killer, Scorpio is a publicity hound, sending cryptic notes to newspapers. He's fully aware that daylight murders in public spaces attract far more attention than those committed in dark alleys at night.

In *Dirty Harry*, the notion of a criminal underworld is upturned, as death comes from above, out of the blue. In the film's opening scene, Scorpio fires from the top of one building (the Bank of America Building at 555 California Street), murdering a woman on the top of another (in the swimming pool on the roof of the Holiday Inn at 750 Kearny Street). Later, the killer's bull's-eye scans crowds in Washington Square Park as he takes aim from the top of Saints Peter and Paul Church (on Filbert Street between Powell and Stockton).

It's fitting, then, that Detective Harry Callahan (Clint Eastwood) first confronts Scorpio in Kezar Stadium, as open a space as one can find in San Francisco. Shot at night, the arena is completely empty, though bright stadium lights give it a ghastly white glare. As the scene ends, the camera flies backward (director Don Siegel shot the sequence from a helicopter), until we can barely distinguish Harry, his foot planted on Scorpio's bloodied chest at the 50-yard line. In a bizarre reversal, the viewer sees the killer from a sniper's perspective.

The closest one can get to that perspective now is to enter Golden Gate Park at Stanyan Boulevard at Beulah Street, walk a block inside the park to the stadium, and climb to the top of the hill on the near side. The original stadium, which was the home of the 49ers from 1946 to 1970 (the year before the film was made), was destroyed in the Loma Prieta earthquake of 1989, but it was rebuilt in the years following and is open to joggers, football and soccer players, and *Dirty Harry* fans fond of asking each other whether they feel lucky, punk.

THE CONVERSATION:
UNION SQUARE

Gene Hackman in *The Conversation*, 1974. Photofest.

Director: Francis Ford Coppola
Cast: Gene Hackman, John Cazale, Allen Garfield, Frederic Forrest
Cinematographer: Bill Butler
American Zoetrope / Paramount Pictures, 1974

UNION SQUARE
Bounded by Post, Geary, Powell, and Stockton Streets

A t one point in *The Conversation*, we learn in passing that surveillance expert Harry Caul (Gene Hackman) had bugged all of a candidate's conversations during a recent presidential campaign. If you work out the dates, it's clear that he's referring to the 1960 race between John F. Kennedy and Richard Nixon. It's a fitting reference, since Harry has an odd affinity with Nixon, who resigned the year *The Conversation* was released. Like Nixon, Harry has made a career out of a paranoid obsession with surveillance, combined with a single-minded determination to succeed—which in Harry's line of work means collecting clear recordings of secret conversations. Where Harry differs from the executive paranoiac is in his attention to the content of the tapes. He couldn't care less what the recorded voices say. As long as the voices are clear and the background noise is minimal, Harry has done his job. That is, until he listens to a conversation he has recorded in Union Square between a nebbish businessman and his secretary.

Union Square is a bugger's worst nightmare. In a scene halfway through the film several surveillance technician colleagues struggle to figure out how Harry managed to record a conversation between a man and woman walking around Union Square, while a reggae band plays and crowds of businesspeople on their lunch hour hold their own competing conversations. Harry, humble as always, does not even point out to his colleagues the job's most difficult challenge: the couple is aware that they might be taped, and are on the watch for any snoops.

The dour, piteous Harry is almost gleeful when he explains to his stumped audience how he used only three microphones to obtain the recording. One of his men carries a microphone in a shopping bag, pattering in and out of range of the couple like any other Union Square eccentric; another perches, sniper-like, on top of the City of Paris department store (now Neiman-Marcus, at 150 Stockton Street), aiming a directional microphone at the couple; the third spy, Harry himself, munches a sandwich and walks near the couple whenever the first man moves out of range. Later, in the editing room, after some deft knob-adjusting and tape-cutting, Harry mixes the three audio tracks together to achieve a perfect recording of the couple's conversation. Maybe too perfect. The couple's conversation, clear-sounding and urgent but of ambiguous meaning, gives Harry an ideal object on which to project his paranoia.

As Harry's interest in the taped conversation grows, so does his paranoia; he comes to believe that he is the victim of a system of surveillance even more sophisticated than his own. And when Harry's paranoia turns inward, director Francis Ford Coppola narrows his focus accordingly. Like Harry in his editing studio, where he gradually refines his chaotic recording of numerous overheard conversations and background noises until he isolates a single conversation, Coppola gradually shifts his focus away from the film's other characters, and even from the details of the plot, until there is nothing left but Harry's maniacal paranoia. Having begun in the crowded, wide-open Union Square, by the final scene we're left alone with Harry in his empty bedroom, as he systematically tears apart the furniture and then the walls. In his crazed state, he believes that he is being bugged, and searches fruitlessly for a hidden microphone.

In early noirs, the actions of the femme fatales and the villains lead the hero into a web of confusion that forces him out of his imagined security. *The Conversation* inverts that typical noir plot: Coppola creates a character who, from the outset, is already paranoid, alienated, alone. (It's revealed early in the film that Harry, fearful of being bugged himself, does not even have a home phone.) The film begins, then, where most classic films noirs end, in despair and paranoia. And it ends not with the hero's defeat by his pursuers, but in a manner that Nixon himself would recognize: self-destruction.

INVASION OF THE
BODY SNATCHERS:
ALAMO SQUARE

Brooke Adams and Donald Sutherland in *Invasion of the Body Snatchers*, 1978. Photofest.

Director: Philip Kaufman
Cast: Donald Sutherland, Brooke Adams, Jeff Goldblum, Veronica Cartwright, Leonard Nimoy
Cinematographer: Michael Chapman
MGM, 1978

ALAMO SQUARE
Bounded by Fulton, Hayes, Steiner, and Scott Streets
POSTCARD ROW
700 block of Steiner Street, between Hayes and Grove Streets
Matthew Kavanaugh, architect
Built in 1895

In director Philip Kaufman's remake of Don Siegel's *Invasion of the Body Snatchers* (1954), alien pods descend on the city of San Francisco, which turns out to be a particularly fertile breeding ground. The pods colonize the city, one snatched body at a time. As in many earlier noirs, the film's plot pits a virtuous public servant (Donald Sutherland) against a vast, amorphous conspiracy that threatens to destroy both him and the woman he loves (Brooke Adams). The more he learns about this conspiracy, the more he isolates himself from his friends, who betray him one by one (especially the shifty Leonard Nimoy). Ultimately he finds himself alone, fighting an impossibly powerful, hidden enemy. As the city slowly closes in on him, paranoia and desperation drive him to previously unimaginable acts of violence.

Stylistically, *Body Snatchers* is one of the most innovative neo-noirs in the ways that it approximates with color film the unnerving, claustrophobic effect of the expressionistic black-and-white familiar from 1940s and '50s noir. Like those earlier films, *Body Snatchers* makes deft use of shadow. Many shots are framed with dark borders, giving the viewer the sense that there is something evil lurking just offscreen (as there often is). Kaufman also frequently shoots from oblique angles, forcing the viewer to suspect that even his most innocuous subjects, such as oblivious passersby or children playing in the park, might in fact be menacing pods. Cinematographer Mark Chapman shot the scenes on the streets of San Francisco with a hidden camera; the crowds on Market Street and the people walking past City Hall are unaware that they are being filmed. It's a measure of the film's success in creating a mood of paranoia that we mistake these innocent San Franciscans for man-slurping aliens.

But Kaufman does more than just approximate these black-and-white techniques. The colors he does use are ugly and menacing. His San Francisco is not an overwhelmingly sinister or dark place; in fact many of the scenes are shot in bright daylight, in open spaces—Union Square, a rooftop in Telegraph Hill, a busy intersection in the Tenderloin, and the plaza in front of City Hall. Yet even the most mundane scenes are tinted with strange extraterrestrial greens and purples, colors that subtly suggest that all is not well in the City, that some kind of grotesque illness is furiously incubating just below the surface.

This ominous foreboding is felt in the very first scene, when biologist Elizabeth Driscoll (Adams) strolls through the park in Alamo Square on her way home from work. As a group of schoolchildren runs by, she pauses to pick a beautiful, exotic red flower. It's a happy, familiar image. But something is terribly wrong. The flower is an unusually bright blood red, and the schoolteacher has a harrowing, twisted expression on her face. The camera then zooms past the teacher and toward the swing set, where we see a priest rocking back and forth on one of the swings. He seems both oddly familiar yet completely incongruous amid the laughing, playing children. As he glares off camera, presumably at Elizabeth, we recognize the priest. His blank, maniacal stare betrays him as a pod person— perhaps San Francisco's first. He is also, we realize, Robert Duvall, in a bizarre and well-timed cameo. Duvall as a creepy priest can only bode ill.

Adding to the eerie wholesomeness of this opening scene, the camera follows Elizabeth as she walks across the street into her house at 720 Steiner Street, on Postcard Row, the picturesque row of old San Francisco Victorian houses bordering Alamo Square. Although some may recognize it from postcards of the city, Postcard Row has now gained greater renown for its appearance in the opening credit sequence of *Full House*—a television show about pods if ever there was one.

HAMMETT:
HAMMETT'S ALLEY APARTMENT

David Patrick Kelly and Frederic Forrest in *Hammett*, 1982. Photofest.

Director: Wim Wenders
Cast: Frederic Forrest, Peter Boyle, Marilu Henner, Jack Nance
Cinematographer: Joseph Biroc
Zoetrope, 1982

DASHIELL HAMMETT'S REAL APARTMENT
891 Post Street, #401
DASHIELL HAMMETT'S APARTMENT IN *HAMMETT*
On Hastings Alley, off of Hyde Street
Back entrance to apartment building at 1184-1188 Union Street

f rancis Ford Coppola made one of the best neo-noirs ever, *The Conversation*, by eschewing overt stylistic homage to classic film noir in order to explore at great depth a single noir theme: paranoia. In *Hammett*, he took the opposite approach, and ended up with the opposite result. Following closely in the tradition of early film noir, he hired a German émigré director (Wim Wenders), shot the film almost entirely on soundstages, invoked Dashiell Hammett wherever possible (Hammett is the main character, the dialogue is cribbed from Hammett's fiction, and the story is a Continental Op knockoff), and even gave cameos to noir stalwarts Sylvia Sydney, Elisha Cook, Jr., and director Sam Fuller. Wenders played along, casting long shadows from lowered Venetian blinds and zigzagging fire escapes across virtually every shot, even when windows were nowhere to be found. The sets are strange and often gorgeous, the rooms painted in garish orange-red, or jaundiced yellow, or celadon; the scenes on the waterfront seem to hover in the mist that peels off the swamp-green Bay. And yet the film fails, and fails badly, since it stumbles on the same problem that plagues all purely nostalgic art: the closer it comes to replicating its original source, the more the strains of imitation show. Hammett does not say things like "People lose teeth talking like that" because he's angry and about to break open a head, but because Sam Spade says it. Marilu Henner's stunning red hair recalls Rita Hayworth's, sort of, but the rest of her does not, and Frederic Forrest, the actor who plays Hammett in the film, is, needless to say, no

Humphrey Bogart—nor for that matter Alan Ladd or even Dana Andrews. *Hammett*'s failure goes to show that the crucial components of film noir are not just style and content, but also context.

One of the very few glimpses we see of the real San Francisco in the film is the alley off of Hyde Street where Hammett lives. The real Hammett did have an apartment off of Hyde, but it was 891 Post Street in the Tenderloin (an address he also used for Sam Spade's apartment in *The Maltese Falcon*). It would be too severe to call this a slip-up, but in a movie that labors so painfully to replicate other equally marginal details of Hammett's life and fiction, this minor transposition stands out like a tarantula on a slice of angel food.

JAGGED EDGE:
BAKER BEACH

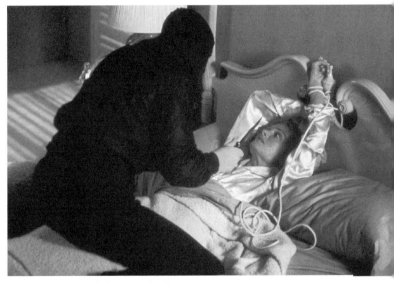

Maria Mayenzet in *Jagged Edge*, 1985. Photofest.

Director: Richard Marquand
Cast: Glenn Close, Jeff Bridges, Peter Coyote
Cinematographer: Matthew F. Leonetti
Columbia Pictures, 1985

BAKER BEACH
Enter at southwest corner
of Gibson Road, off Lincoln Boulevard

After the opening credits roll over the requisite shot of the Golden Gate Bridge, with the San Francisco skyline hazy behind it, the clichés come, as Joe Eszterhas might put it, hot and heavy: a beach house on a cliff at night; a thunderstorm; dissonant synthesizer chords; a masked killer creeping up the stairs and slowly turning the doorknob to the master bedroom, where a woman lies asleep; a rope, a knife, and a bloodcurdling scream; close-up of woman's eyes opening very wide; close-up of raised knife's JAGGED EDGE. The most subtle thing about *Jagged Edge* is, in fact, its title.

The murder victim, we soon find out, is the heiress of a San Francisco newspaper-publishing family (not Hearst, but "Lofton"), whose entire fortune will pass upon her death to her raffish, philandering husband Jack Forrester (Jeff Bridges). Jack is the obvious suspect, and as the investigation continues, other circumstantial evidence comes to light that seems to implicate him. Enter Teddy Barnes (Glenn Close), a virtuous public-prosecutor-turned-defense-lawyer. She decides to save Jack, whom she firmly believes is innocent (and sexy).

Screenwriter Joe Ezsterhas excels in writing plots that are so deliberate and consummately clichéd that any deviation from the obvious seems subversive. He is a master of the red herring that is not a red herring, of reverse psychology, of the clue so damning that one discounts it out of hand. In more conventional whodunit murder mysteries, nothing is what it seems. The initial suspect never turns out to be guilty. In *Jagged Edge*, on the other hand, everything is what it seems. The main suspect turns out to be the killer, and the D.A.'s initial hunches are proven correct. Again and again in Ezsterhas' films, the viewer is surprised—or at least bemused—by the outcome that he most expected.

The one thing in *Jagged Edge* that is not what it seems is Baker Beach, the site of the heiress' murder. Although the Forresters' weekend beach house appears to stand isolated in a hidden cove somewhere in Marin County, the real Baker Beach is not especially secluded; it is located in San Francisco proper, in the Presidio, just north of the Sea Cliff neighborhood, and just to the west of the Golden Gate Bridge. The Bay's powerful rip currents make for thrilling (if life-endangering) swimming. A sign cautions beachgoers against coming in contact with the ocean, ominously warning that "People swimming and wading have drowned here." But the beach's main attraction is its view of the Golden Gate, the most beautiful view of the bridge in the city. For a more intimate view of the Golden Gate—and of your fellow sunbathers—walk north on the mile-long-beach toward the bridge. The brown-and-yellow "Hazardous Surf" sign unofficially marks the beginning of the nudist area, which the *San Francisco Bay Guardian* perennially awards the coveted prize of San Francisco's Best Nude Beach.

PACIFIC HEIGHTS:
THE HOUSE FROM HELL

Matthew Modine and Melanie Griffith in *Pacific Heights*, 1990. Photofest.

Director: John Schlesinger
Cast: Michael Keaton, Melanie Griffith, Matthew Modine
Cinematographer: Amir M. Mokri
Morgan Creek, 1990

THE HOUSE FROM HELL
1243 19th Street at Texas Street

f ollowing (albeit tenuously) in the tradition of *The House on Telegraph
Hill* comes *Pacific Heights*, a late addition to that most arcane of noir
subgenres, the Real Estate Noir. These films are not to be confused with
haunted-house horror films, although they have in common with them
the creeping sense that there is something terrible lurking under the ele-
gant gables and behind the spotless picture windows. And just as earlier
noirs capture much of the anxiety about issues contemporary to their
time, *Pacific Heights* exploits the most dreaded source of terror for early-
1990s upwardly mobile professionals: the real estate market.

Screenwriter Daniel Pyne based the plot of the film on his own experience as a landlord burdened with an unruly tenant who refused to pay
the rent. He could hardly have picked a better setting for his screenplay
than San Francisco, notorious for being the worst real estate market in
the country, both in terms of availability and cost (the average price of a
home in San Francisco is now over $2.3 million). Here real estate is dis-
cussed in the same hushed, nervous tones that are used to discuss alco-
holism in Las Vegas or car-jacking in Miami. Available real estate, especially in upscale neighborhoods, is so hard to come by that even the
film's producers could not find a property in the real Pacific Heights to
rent for filming. Instead they settled on a Victorian house in the modest,
and more affordable, Potrero Hill.

As Drake Goodman (Matthew Modine) and Patty Palmer (Melanie
Griffith) discover in *Pacific Heights*, evicting a tenant in San Francisco is

a daunting proposition. Especially when the tenant is the demonic con man Carter Hayes, played with maniacal ardor by Michael Keaton. Hayes' scam is to move into a new apartment, systematically dismantle it, refuse to pay rent, and then, after being violently evicted, sue the landlord for violation of the lease agreement. The premise is something of a San Francisco in-joke, since the city's rent laws provide the tenant with a level of legal protection unparalleled in virtually any other American city. What's terrifying, especially to viewers who may happen to be San Francisco landowners, is not simply the wickedness of Hayes' scheme, but the fact that it works.

This uneven relationship between real estate owners and tenants is part of a tradition that dates back to an incident involving one of the city's most famous landowners, the railroad titan Charles Crocker. Like the other members of the Big Four responsible for building the Central Pacific Railroad—Leland Stanford, Mark Hopkins, and Collis Huntington—Crocker sought to build a mansion on Nob Hill a full square block in size. In 1877, he bought up a dozen houses on the block between California and Sacramento, Jones and Taylor (now the site of Grace Cathedral), generously compensating the previous landowners and helping them to secure new homes. Only Nicholas Yung, a German undertaker, refused to sell his house. Instead he asked for $6,000 (roughly $100,000 today), over three times what Crocker had paid for the other houses. Crocker reluctantly agreed to the sum. Whereupon Yung upped his asking price to $12,000. Deeply perturbed, Crocker agreed again. At which point Yung raised his price to $40,000. Crocker decided to go ahead with his house anyway; instead of building over Yung's property, he would build around it.

Crocker surrounded Yung's property on three sides with a forty-foot-high wooden wall, blocking the undertaker's view of the Bay (and of everything else, except for the street in front of his house). Local activists rallied against Crocker's "spite fence," lighting bonfires and pounding against it with their fists. Yung, likely as disturbed by the angry mobs as Crocker, finally sold his house for $6,000 several months later and relocated. It took another, much bigger, fire to destroy the Crocker mansion, which collapsed during the earthquake of 1906.

FINAL ANALYSIS:
PIGEON POINT LIGHT
STATION / BATTERY SPENCER

Richard Gere and Kim Basinger in *Final Analysis*, 1992. Photofest.

Director: Phil Joanou
Cast: Richard Gere, Kim Basinger, Uma Thurman
Cinematographer: Jordan Cronenweth
Warner Bros., 1992

BATTERY SPENCER
On Conzelman Road, first turn-in after exit off of U.S. 101

In the early 1990s Kim Basinger was offered a leading role in two films that were to be shot at the same time. The first film was a noir thriller set in San Francisco, in which she would play a mysterious blond femme fatale. The woman kills her gangster boyfriend with a common household item but beats the murder rap with the help of an innocent lawman whom she has seduced and manipulated, employing intricate mind games that play on his deepest insecurities and desires. The script was heavy with tortuous plot twists, graphic sex, and overt references to Alfred Hitchcock's *Vertigo*. She turned it down. The movie was called *Basic Instinct* and the role went to a relatively unknown actress named Sharon Stone.

Instead Basinger took a part in the second film, also a noir thriller set in San Francisco, in which she would play a mysterious blond femme fatale. The woman kills her gangster husband with a common household item but beats the murder rap with the help of an innocent legal psychologist whom she has seduced and manipulated, employing intricate mind games that play on his deepest insecurities and desires. The script was heavy with tortuous plot twists, graphic sex, and overt references to Alfred Hitchcock's *Vertigo*. It was called *Final Analysis*. It was not a good decision.

Despite these similarities *Final Analysis* does not nearly reach the diabolical cleverness and ironic sense of humor of Paul Verhoeven's excellent and underappreciated film. One needs look no further than the films' choice of murder weapon. *Basic Instinct*'s ice pick chips away at a mystery as prismatic as a glacier, shaping bizarre, glittering ice sculptures along the way. *Final Analysis*' barbell, on the other hand, clobbers viewers on the head over and over again until they're ready to fall face forward into a bathtub.

Along with the barbell murder scene, the film's two most memorable scenes take place at a tall lighthouse that appears in the film to stand just east of the Golden Gate on the Marin County side. Like the bell tower at Mission San Juan Bautista in *Vertigo*, this lighthouse appears twice. Dr. Isaac Barr (Richard Gere) takes a gangster's wife, Heather Evans (Basinger), there on a romantic excursion early in the film. They return in the film's climactic scene, when Basinger takes her Kim Novak-inspired fall from the top of the tower, while Gere dangles from the broken railing in a shot that aspires to emulate the opening scene of *Vertigo*, in which Jimmy Stewart hangs helplessly off the edge of an apartment building.

The lighthouse does exist, but it is fifty miles south of San Francisco, (not far from Mission San Juan Bautista) off of Highway 1. The 115-foot Pigeon Point Light Station, which opened in 1872, is one of the tallest lighthouses in America. In a coincidence as strange as any of those which keep cropping up in *Final Analysis*, a section of the cornice on the exterior of the lighthouse fell off in 2001. In the film, the same thing happens, bringing the catwalk (and Heather) down with it.

The last exit ramp off of Highway 101 before the Golden Gate on the Marin side leads straight up to a bluff that is almost even in height with the top of the bridge's first tower. There are parking spots available right off of the winding road, and a path leads up a small incline toward the ocean. In a recession hidden in the hillside are the barracks, gun emplacements, and commander's station of Battery Spencer. The U.S. military operated this strategically positioned post between 1897 and 1943, its enormous M1888 twelve-inch breech-loading rifles guarding the opening of the Bay. Standing at the edge of the bluff on a clear day you can see the city's skyline and the Presidio, Alcatraz and the Bay, the yawning Pacific, the Bay Bridge, and of course the Golden Gate, which seems within the range of a hard-thrown stone. A better time to go, however, is at dawn when the fog is at its thickest. When the sun rises, it's impossible to make out Battery Spencer; only the blue fog, which completely obscures the Bay and all of San Francisco, gradually turns white. The top of the near tower vanishes, as does the rest of the Golden Gate, mid-cable. The few cars on the bridge at that early hour drive to a certain point and then disappear. The foreshortened bridge appears to hover above the Bay, vague and disembodied.

BASIC INSTINCT:
DETECTIVE NICK
CURRAN'S APARTMENT

Sharon Stone and Michael Douglas in
Basic Instinct, 1992. Photofest.

Director: Paul Verhoeven
Cast: Michael Douglas, Sharon Stone
Cinematographer: Jan de Bont
Carolco Pictures / TriStar Pictures, 1992

DETECTIVE NICK CURRAN'S APARTMENT
1158-1170 Montgomery Street
at Green Street

B *asic Instinct* is most famous for a certain shot in which Sharon Stone's character, Catherine Tramell, pulls off the classic liar's pantomime: the show-and-not-tell. She doesn't tell the detectives anything helpful about their investigation into the murder of an old San Francisco rock star, but she shows them, well, everything. There is another startling aspect to this scene, however, less titillating sexually than cinematically. When Detective Nick Curran (Michael Douglas) stops by her house in Stinson Beach to take her downtown for the interrogation, Catherine asks him to wait while she changes into something "more appropriate" for a police interrogation. She emerges from her bedroom in a sleeveless white mini-dress, with her bleached hair pulled back into a bun: the spitting image of Madeleine Elster (Kim Novak) in *Vertigo*. In fact all of Stone's dresses were designed to match Novak's outfits in *Vertigo*, and she wears them in the same order as they appear in that earlier film.

Basic Instinct is, in many ways besides sartorially, a re-imagining of *Vertigo*. Both begin with a similar premise. A detective, shaky from a recent failure on the job, becomes obsessed by a case involving an alluring, mysterious woman. He trails her around San Francisco, searching for clues that might disclose her real identity, and finds himself falling in love with her. The detective also has a brainy, but sexually repressed, female confidant whose romantic advances he spurns in favor of the far more erotic promise of an affair with the mysterious woman. Ultimately he finds himself questioning his most basic moral and investigative assumptions as he falls headlong into a dark conspiracy beyond his own control.

The similarities of plot between the two films seem negligible, however, when compared to similarities in the films' technique and style. Director Paul Verhoeven makes constant, even obsessive, use of *Vertigo*'s doubling motif. *Vertigo* begins with the strange case of a woman, Madeleine Elster, who is fixated on, and may be possessed by, an ancestor, Carlotta Valdes, who committed suicide a century earlier. After Madeleine kills herself, Scottie vainly seeks to reenact his affair and atone for his failure to prevent Madeleine's death by recruiting Judy, a woman who resembles Madeleine, to act as the dead woman's reincarnation. Scottie imagines that through Judy, he will be able to experience again his former happiness, but he doesn't realize that by doing so, he is also fated to relive the tragedy of her death.

Basic Instinct also begins with a doubling: the first murder occurs in exactly the same way as it does in a novel called, fittingly, *Love Hurts*. Catherine, the author of the novel, instantly becomes the main suspect in the case. As the police psychologist points out, either the killer is a copycat of the novel's killer, a double of a fictional character, or the killer is Catherine, acting out the plot of her own novel. When Nick shows up at Catherine's house to talk to her the morning after the murder, he finds a woman matching her physical description, only to discover that she is not Catherine, but Roxy, her friend (and lover, we later discover). Many other doppelgängers emerge, but the film's most dramatic doubling is between Catherine and Nick. In an infinitely recursive plot twist, Catherine announces that she is modeling the main character of her next novel after Nick. In her book, she tells him, the detective falls for the wrong woman. Nick asks her what happens in the end. "He dies," she says. Whenever Nick interrogates her about the murders, she fires the same questions back at him, needling him about his supposedly accidental shooting of several tourists during a police chase. "We're both innocent," she says at one point, meaning, perhaps, the opposite.

Several murders later, Nick himself becomes a prime suspect and is brought in for questioning. Much of the dialogue is repeated verbatim from the earlier interrogation scene, only this time Nick answers the questions instead of asking them. Somewhat surprisingly, he clearly enjoys affecting Catherine's personality, and cockily evading the detectives' accusations. Soon he's even bought his own ice pick.

The effect of this doubling technique—in which whole scenes are repeated over and over, shot by shot—is to create an expectation that past horrors never go away, but are ultimately bound to resurface, with tragic consequences. Just as in *Vertigo*, each act of doubling only confirms this eerie symmetry. It's fitting, then, that the film has two endings. In what seems to be the last scene, Catherine lies in bed with Nick, apparently having decided to live with him. As Nick speaks optimistically about their future together (with dialogue repeated from an earlier scene), Catherine menacingly stretches her arm towards the edge of the mattress. But when she pulls her hand away it is empty, and the two embrace. The screen fades to black: a happy ending. Yet a moment later, we're back in the bedroom. Verhoeven leaves the entangled couple behind and slowly pans down to reveal the ice pick beneath the mattress.

Nick's apartment building is on the corner of Montgomery and Green. Unfortunately the apartment's spiral staircase, an overt reference to the dizzying staircase in the church bell tower at Mission San Juan Bautista in *Vertigo*, was built for the film. (1158–1170 Montgomery does actually have a stairway in the middle of the apartment building, but it lacks the open drop between the spiraling staircases.) Yet even in this detail is Verhoeven consistent with the original. The staircase at Mission San Juan Bautista did not exist either. In fact, the Mission does not have a bell tower at all—it was created with special effects.

JADE:
THE PAGODA THEATRE

Linda Fiorentino in *Jade*, 1995. Photofest.

Director: William Friedkin
Cast: David Caruso, Linda Fiorentino, Chazz Palminteri
Cinematographer: Andrzej Bartkowiak
Paramount Pictures, 1995

THE PAGODA THEATRE
1741 Powell Street at the corner of Columbus Avenue

ritics excoriated *Jade* at the time of its release, naming among its faults gratuitous violence, gratuitous sleaze, a lackluster ending, silly dialogue, misuse of Linda Fiorentino in a thin role, and use of David Caruso in a role. But the most vituperative criticism was reserved for screenwriter Joe Eszterhas, whose paychecks so routinely appear in print alongside the names of his scripts that they risk being mistaken for subtitles: *Basic Instinct* ($3 million), *Sliver* ($3 million), *Showgirls* ($2 million), and *Jade* ($2.5 million—for a four-page treatment). His script for *Jade* wasn't only embarrassing, critics complained, but it repeated the errors of his previous scripts. In the *Los Angeles Times*, Kenneth Turan wrote that "his script baldly rips off his earlier *Basic Instinct*"; Roger Ebert huffed that *Jade* "makes the same mistake as *Jagged Edge*"; and the *New York Times'* Janet Maslin chastised Eszterhas for "recycling his own work." They're not wrong. Much of the dialogue is familiar, as is the basic plot (an investigator becomes sexually involved with the lead suspect in a string of sex murders). Whole scenes are plucked intact from his other films. The film's opening sequence, in which a millionaire is murdered in his bedroom by a mysterious killer, replicates the first scenes of both *Basic Instinct* and *Jagged Edge*.

Originality was never Eszterhas' strength. But crass imitation was never a weakness, either. Although his moments of self-plagiarism in *Jade* do evoke a dull sensation of deja vu, the film's most exciting scenes are borrowed from other people's films, and for the most part earlier San

143

Francisco noirs. Only here they are rendered in Eszterhas' typically hyperbolic style: faster, bigger, and louder. At the top of a hill (the script puts him on Divisadero Street, at Broadway—the hill with the sharpest drop in San Francisco), Caruso's brakes suddenly stop working. He speeds down a series of slopes, gaining momentum until his car flies off the road and lands a triple toe-loop onto Lombard Street. It's less frightening, but more spectacular, than a similar scene in *The House on Telegraph Hill*, in which Valentina Cortese flies all the way down Telegraph Hill after *her* car's brake line has been cut. Later in the film Eszterhas forces his plot through the most absurd contortions in order to restage the scene from *The Lady from Shanghai* in which Orson Welles and Rita Hayworth hide out from the cops in a Chinatown theater. In order to set this scenario up, Eszterhas has high-class prostitute Patrice Jacinto (the towering redheaded model Angie Everhart) work as the single non-Chinese hair stylist in a cramped Chinatown hair salon. (Isn't one of the perks of high-class prostitution that you don't have to work in a hair salon?) When Caruso's character, assistant district attorney David Corelli, tries to question her about the murder, she takes off on a headlong sprint through Chinatown alleys and fire escapes and finally into a theater, during a performance by a Chinese dance troupe. In *The Lady from Shanghai*, Welles and Hayworth sit quietly and inconspicuously in the dark theater, waiting for the cops to move on. In *Jade*, Everhart dashes through the backstage dressing rooms, stiff-arming the shrieking, costumed Chinese performers. It's not the last time Chinatown will be inconvenienced by Corelli's chases. The film's most famous scene is a car chase that recalls, inevitably, the famous chase scene in *Bullitt*, only here the cars catapult over the hills, soaring about ten times as high as Steve McQueen's Mustang fastback ever does. The scene reaches its denouement on Grant Avenue in Chinatown, where both cars weave slowly through a parade, crushing Chinese fruit stands, parade floats, and people.

For much of the last century, Chinatown had four great old theaters. Due in large part to the influx of new multiplexes, these old one-screen neighborhood theaters have all closed. Three are currently being used as shopping centers: the Sunsing Theater, the theater in *The Lady from Shanghai*, at 1021 Grant Avenue; the Bella Union at 720 Washington Street, which opened in 1911 as the Shanghai; and the Grandview at

756 Jackson Street. The Great Star Theater at 630 Jackson Street still exists, but was abandoned after closing down in 2002. Built in 1925, the Great Star hosted Chinese opera troupes in its early years and later showed Chinese films until it closed.

Friedkin shot the theater portion of the chase scene from *Jade* with a handheld camera in a single day in the Pagoda, which, despite its name, is not located in Chinatown but nearby in North Beach. The theater, which was built in 1909, closed at the end of 1994, just after this scene was filmed. The building still stands, although entire sections of plaster have fallen off, revealing loose bricks and wooden splints that strain to keep the structure from collapsing altogether. The sign tower, which was added in the late 1930s, still clings precariously to the corner of the building, the only visible indication of the theater's lost identity. Neighborhood merchants and residents thwarted initial plans to convert the Pagoda into a gigantic Rite Aid upon its closing, but it has stood dormant and forgotten ever since.

THE GAME:
THE GARDEN COURT AT
THE PALACE HOTEL

Michael Douglas in *The Game*, 1997. Photofest.

Director: David Fincher
Cast: Michael Douglas, Sean Penn, Deborah Unger
Cinematographer: Harris Savides
Polygram Filmed Entertainment, 1997

THE PALACE HOTEL
2 New Montgomery Street at Market Street
☎ (415) 512-1111

A company called Consumer Recreations Services (CRS) has created a game that promises its wealthy patrons an elaborate role-playing adventure, though its spokesmen are reluctant to disclose any details to prospective players. Investment banking executive Nicholas van Orton (Michael Douglas, who also played a San Francisco "Nick" in *Basic Instinct*) is lured into the elaborate, interactive game by his brother Conrad (Sean Penn) but told little about what will happen to him. Before long he believes a nefarious anonymous organization bent on world domination is draining his bank accounts, vandalizing his house, turning his friends and family against him, and trying to kill him. He is shot at by machine-gun-toting gangsters, is locked in a taxicab that crashes into the Bay, and finally, after being slipped a Mickey, he wakes up in a coffin in a Mexican graveyard. It's paranoia, violence, and betrayal, and it's all in good fun.

The only problem is that "good fun" is hardly any fun at all. Unlike earlier noirs, very little is ultimately at stake. After all, Nick has no real friends or committed relationships, so there's no one whose life he particularly holds dear—not even his own. The only thing he has to lose at the film's outset is his rotten personality. By the end of the film, the game has become nothing more than an expensive therapy session, combining hypnosis, primal scream therapy, suggestive techniques for memory recovery, medication, emotional confrontation with loved ones, forgiveness therapy, and even, in one scene, a Rorschach test.

147

The game warns Nick about the dangers of wealth although, ironically, it is his wealth that gets him into it, and to which he happily returns at the end, to the clink of champagne glasses. It is appropriate then that the party celebrating his birthday, and his completion of the game, is held at the Palace Hotel, a San Francisco landmark famous for both its over-reaching opulence and its dark past. It was built by William Ralston, an Ohioan carpenter who came to San Francisco with the gold-rushers in 1849 and became president of the Bank of California. He invested in various local businesses and building projects, though his greatest aspiration was to construct a grand hotel that would reflect the wealth and pride of his new city. It would cost $5 million (the equivalent of roughly $7.6 billion today), a sum Ralston would finance by dipping into (or rather, emptying) the coffers of the Bank of California, which he had at his disposal. He even dispatched an architect to Europe to study the finest hotels there, so that he might design one that would trump them all. In 1875, just weeks before the hotel was set to open, a local newspaper ran an investigative piece reporting Ralston's creative financing schemes, and the bank's depositors rushed to pull out all of their savings. One of these depositors was the saloon magnate James Flood, whose request to withdraw his entire $6 million account the bank could not satisfy. Ralston was forced to resign the next morning. That afternoon he left for his daily swim in the Bay off of North Beach, in the direction of Alcatraz. He did not return, and the next day his bloated corpse was found floating in the Bay. Although he reportedly died from a stroke, many suspect that he had planned to drown himself.

After the 1906 fire, the Palace Hotel closed for three years, during which time it underwent a full restoration. It opened again with a new addition, the Garden Court, the grand ballroom that serves as the site of Nick's birthday party. It remains just as it appears in the film, with gold leaf sconces, marble columns, two dozen "Austrian" crystal chandeliers, and the pale blue stained-glass ceiling which Nick crashes through after jumping from the hotel's roof. Douglas, of course, did not actually fall through the ceiling; the shattered glass is a trick of computer animation. (The cost of repairing the ceiling would have alone doubled the film's budget.) Veteran hotel staffers enjoy recalling how Douglas fell from a platform just a wee three feet above the thick landing pad. The Garden

Court is available for private events of 75 to 1,000 people, and is open to the public daily for breakfast, lunch and, on Sundays, brunch. For those who wish to have the real van Orton experience, the Garden Court offers an Exclusive Tea for Two for $85.

TWISTED:
TOSCA CAFÉ

Andy Garcia and Ashley Judd in *Twisted*, 2004. Photofest.

Director: Philip Kaufman
Cast: Ashley Judd, Samuel L. Jackson, Andy Garcia
Cinematographer: Peter Deming
Paramount Pictures, 2004

TOSCA CAFÉ
242 Columbus Avenue between Broadway
and Pacific Avenue
☎ (415) 391-1244

Twisted revives one of film noir's rarest, and most peculiar plot devices: the mystery drug. In *D.O.A.* (1950) Edmund O'Brien discovers that he's been poisoned with the fluorescent "luminous toxin"; in *Decoy* (1946), Jean Gillie discovers that "methylene blue" can be used as an antidote to cyanide poisoning; and in the obscure Czech Gothic-noir *Morgiana* (1971), a girl uses a slow-acting hallucinogen to kill her sister, only to discover that the toxin's effects are contagious. As in these other films, the strange properties of the drug in *Twisted* explain aspects of the plot that would otherwise be nonsensical. The one difference is that in *Twisted*, the drug is a real one.

Homicide detective Jessica Shepard (Ashley Judd) has a drinking problem: whenever she gets drunk, someone dies. More specifically, whenever she gets drunk, she sleeps with a stranger, blacks out, and awakens to find her sex partner murdered. As the detective assigned to the case, she's her own lead suspect. A scrupulous investigator, Shepard has her own blood tested (though, rather unscrupulously, she doesn't do so until three men are dead). She tests positive for rohypnol, the notorious date-rape drug. Commonly known as "roofies," the colorless and tasteless drug dissolves quickly in liquids and causes extreme fatigue and blackouts that begin within thirty minutes of ingestion and generally last for twelve hours. Even methylene blue is powerless against it.

Shepard begins drinking early in the film, at a party held in honor of her promotion to the homicide department at the Tosca Café in North

Beach. Tosca, which Nick Curran and his cop friends frequent in *Basic Instinct*, is a dim yellow-lit bar with dark red leather booths and Formica tables, a black-and-red checkered floor, an old jukebox that plays Dean Martin or Luciano Pavarotti for a quarter, and hat-trees left over from the days when gentlemen wore fedoras. Framed playbills from old performances of Puccini's *Tosca* line the wall, sharing space with an enormous, browning mural of the Grand Canal in Venice and an original poster for *The Lady from Shanghai*. Tosca's specialty drink is a house cappuccino, which is laced with nothing more toxic than a shot of house brandy.

THE ANNUAL NOIR CITY
FILM FESTIVAL

H alfway through *The Velvet Touch*, a 1948 Broadway noir starring Rosalind Russell and Claire Trevor, a rotund, friendly policeman ambles onto the set of a New York theater to investigate the murder of producer Gordon Dunning (Leon Ames), who has been clobbered to death by his own award statuette. The crowd in the palatial Castro Theatre, filled to its 1,600-seat capacity, rocks with applause. A novice might smile uncertainly at this unexpected outburst but the mumbled asides in the rows around him will soon let him in on the cause for celebration: the man onscreen is Sydney Greenstreet, the amiable character actor most famous for his turn as the short-winded mastermind Kasper Gutman in *The Maltese Falcon*. Like Victor Sen Young, Edmond O'Brien, and Lee J. Cobb, or for that matter Robert Mitchum, Alan Ladd, Richard Conte, Robert Ryan, Richard Widmark, and Robert Taylor—and don't forget Joan Crawford, Barbara Stanwyck, Rita Hayworth, Ida Lupino, Lizabeth Scott, Gloria Grahame, Ann Sheridan, and many, many others—he is a fan favorite.

Noir City Film Festival is the most successful film noir festival in the world because it is attended by the world's most avid film noir fans. In just its second year (2004), it had become the most successful film series at the Castro—no small feat. (In 2005 the series was held at the Balboa Theater in the Richmond District.) Hosted by local noir impresario Eddie Muller, who dons his most dapper white suit for the occasion, the festival expanded in 2004 to a two-week run (with two-for-one double features every day). Each year has a different theme: in 2003, it was San Francisco noir (all films shown in that series are included in this book);

153

2004 was dedicated to the women of noir: vixens, vamps, and victims. The festival's gala opening night featured a screening of *Detour*, followed by a conversation with the film's star, Ann Savage.

The festival tends to feature both popular noir classics, like *Double Indemnity*, *The Lady from Shanghai*, and *The Postman Always Rings Twice*, as well as curiosities like *The Accused*, *Desert Fury*, and *Edge of Doom*, some of which have not been seen on the big screen in decades. At last year's festival, it was the rare (and regretful) moviegoer that did not stay for both parts of a double feature. Noir addicts came to recognize each other, especially since many sat in the same seats for every screening. By the end of the festival, a certain camaraderie developed among those in the theater—a shared feeling of world-weariness, popcorn stupor, and wonderment.

THE DANGER AND DESPAIR KNITTING CIRCLE

Thursday Night Screenings
Secret locations
www.noirfilm.com

A cross between a film society and a speakeasy, the Danger and Despair Knitting Circle is the black heart of San Francisco's noir underworld. Led by "Dark" Marc Dolezal and film collector Paul Meienberg, the Knitting Circle is a non-profit organization that has amassed a nearly comprehensive film noir library, containing more than 700 titles. They sell and trade their tapes and DVDs to noir fanatics all over the world, and donate them to universities, scholars, and libraries. They also run several film series over the course of the year. One recent series focused on Poverty Row noirs ("B" films made on shoestring budgets by studios like Monogram and Lippert Pictures), for which the Circle unearthed 16mm prints of *City on a Hunt*, *Treasure of Monte Cristo*, and the bizarre ice-skating noir, *Suspense*. A series on the Red Scare included films like *I*

Was a Communist for the F.B.I. and *I Married a Communist*, while "Film Noir of 1941: The Gateway Year" inspired lively debates about the origins of film noir.

These screenings are not entirely open to the public, however. To gain admission you must email Dark Marc, who will reserve you a spot in the crowded downtown screening room (audiences usually number over fifty). He'll happily slip you the address of that week's secret location—that is, so long as you're on the level.

Distinguished noir scholars often act as guest hosts, introducing the films and leading discussion sessions after each screening. Common topics include the merits of the flashback and the voice-over, the scandalous private life of a certain diva, and most importantly, the degree to which the film under discussion could be considered "noir." These discussions often lead to a debate over the very definition of film noir itself. Charitably priced booze and popcorn are made available while regulars quiz the audience with such stingers as: "What is the name of the actor who played Chang?" or "What was the address of the mental asylum?" or "What kind of lipstick did Adele Jergens wear?" (Answers: Victor Sen Yung, 2015 Franklin Street, and Orange Blossom). Winners receive VHS copies of rare noir classics like *Decoy* and *Subway in the Sky*.

The Knitting Circle proudly treats even the campiest, most obscure films as treasures, and actresses like Vera Ralston and Belita receive a level of respect usually reserved for Marlene and Joan. While much of this adoration is tempered with irony, the respect accorded to each film is justified. After all, many of the films screened by this small group have not been seen in decades, and will likely not be seen again for years. The Knitting Circle members enjoy the high camp and the melodrama, but they take the films, and their knowledge of them, seriously, since without their efforts, many of these films would simply cease to exist. Many already have. Prints of old "B" films are usually poorly preserved and have an alarming tendency to vanish into the dark holds of abandoned vaults in the back lots of Hollywood studios. The members of the Knitting Circle—both the film collectors who unearth rare prints of lost films, and the audience that comes to enjoy them—are more than connoisseurs. They are the proud custodians of film noir's legacy.

SELECTED BIBLIOGRAPHY

Adams, Charles F. *The Magnificent Rogues of San Francisco: A Gallery of Fakers and Frauds, Rascals and Robber Barons, Scoundrels and Scalawags.* Palo Alto, California: Pacific Books, 1998.

Asbury, Herbert. *The Barbary Coast: An Informal History of the San Francisco Underworld.* New York: Alfred A. Knopf, 1933.

Bacon, Daniel. *Walking San Francisco on the Barbary Coast Trail.* San Francisco: Quicksilver Press, 1996.

Blaisdell, Marilyn. *San Francisciana: Photographs of Sutro Baths.* San Francisco: Marilyn Blaisdell, 1987.

Borde, Raymond and Etienne Chaumeton. *A Panorama of American Film Noir.* San Francisco: City Lights Books, 2002 (Paul Hammond, translator).

Brechin, Grey. "1360 Montgomery," *Metro.* September 1981.

Caen, Herb. *Herb Caen's Guide to San Francisco.* Garden City, NY: Doubleday & Company, Inc., 1957. With drawings by Earl Thollander.

Christopher, Nicholas. *Somewhere in the Night: Film Noir and the American City.* New York: The Free Press, 1997.

Driscoll, Marjorie C. "Golden Gate Theater Opened With Record Crowds," *San Francisco Chronicle*, March 27, 1922.

Heritage Newsletter, Fall 1983. "Beloved Old Building Is a Beauty Once Again."

Hogan, William and William German, eds. *The San Francisco Chronicle Reader.* New York: McGraw-Hill Book Company, Inc., 1962.

Keegan, Timothy. "1360 Montgomery Street," *Panorama.* October–December 2001.

Kraft, Jeff and Aaron Leventhal. *Footsteps in the Fog: Alfred Hitchcock's San*

Francisco. Santa Monica: Santa Monica Press, 2002.

Lloyd, B.E. *Lights and Shades in San Francisco*. San Francisco: A.L. Bancroft & Company, 1876.

Meyer, David N. *A Girl and a Gun: The Complete Guide to Film Noir on Video*. New York: Avon Books, 1998.

Muller, Eddie. *Dark City: The Lost World of Film Noir*. New York: St. Martin's Press, 1998.

Nunan, Thomas. "Golden Gate Theater Opens Its Alluring Doors," *San Francisco Examiner*, March 27, 1992, p.10.

Purdy, Helen Throop. *San Francisco: As It Was, As It Is, And How to See It*. San Francisco: Paul Elder and Company Publishers, 1912.

Rapp, Frank. "The Golden Gate," Pictorial Brochure, April, 1965, Page H. Richards, Rand. *Historic Walks in San Francisco: 18 Trails Through the City's Past*. San Francisco: Heritage House Publishers, 2001.

Riesenberg, Frank, Jr. *Golden Gate: The Story of San Francisco Harbor*. New York: Knopf, 1940.

Silver, Alain and James Ursini, eds. *Film Noir Reader*. New York: Limelight Editions, 1996.

Thomson, David. *The New Biographical Dictionary of Film*. New York: Knopf, 2002.

Thomson, David. *Rosebud: The Story of Orson Welles*. New York: Knopf, 1996.

Dr. Weirde's Weirde Tours: A Guide to Mysterious San Francisco. San Francisco: Barrett-James Books, 1994.

www.mistersf.com

www.norcalmovies.com

INDEX

ACKNOWLEDGEMENTS

I'm greatly indebted to "Dark" Marc Dolezal and the Danger and Despair Knitting Circle for their generosity in providing me with many of the films included in this book from their voluminous library, an excellent resource for anyone interested in film noir. Philip Kaufman, Peter Kaufman, David Thomson, and Eddie Muller magnanimously shared with me their valuable insights on film noir and on San Francisco film in general. Robin Straus was extremely kind to volunteer her expertise in the project's initial phase. The staff of the San Francisco History Center at the San Francisco Public Library and Stacy Wisnia at the Castro Theatre gave me important assistance in my research for the book. Borden Elniff put on the finishing touches. I'm most grateful to my publisher, Angela Hederman, for her trust and support and my editor, Nadia Aguiar, whose dedication, editorial acuity, and enthusiasm have guided the project since its conception.

ABOUT THE AUTHOR

Nathaniel Rich has written for *The Los Angeles Times*, *The Nation*, *Slate*, and *The New Republic*. He lives in San Francisco.